WHAT THE SPIRIT SAYS TO THE CHURCHES

A Commentary on Revelation 1-3

ANDREW J. LINDSEY

WESTBOW°
PRESS
A DIVISION OF THOMAS NELSON
& ZONDERVAN

WestBow Press books may be ordered through
booksellers or by contacting:

WestBow Press
A Division of Thomas Nelson & Zondervan
1663 Liberty Drive
Bloomington, IN 47403
www.westbowpress.com
1 (866) 928-1240

ISBN: 978-1-4908-3811-3 (sc)

Library of Congress Control Number: 2014909388

Printed in the United States of America.

WestBow Press rev. date: 07/30/2014

Contents

Dedicated to the elders of Grace
Heritage Church in Auburn, AL–
Paul Stith and Stan Reeves: faithful pastors,
who provided the first formal setting in
which I began to learn biblical Greek–
and to Dr. Daniel Hatfield– pastor of
Audubon Baptist Church in Louisville,
KY and former professor at the Southern
Baptist Theological Seminary–
who faithfully taught me biblical Greek
and helped to further excite my passion
for Revelation 1-3.

It is my goal in writing this work to render a commentary on Revelation 1-3 that is clear, concise, accurate, and Christ-focused.

In ten chapters, I touch upon each of the major points raised in the first three chapters of Revelation. Each chapter of this work begins with my translation of the verses under consideration. My translation admittedly lacks a certain smoothness, as it is focused (for the most part) on yielding a literal, word-for-word translation of the Greek text.

This commentary is divided into two major parts. Part One of this commentary focuses on Revelation Chapter 1, introducing the human author of this work (the Apostle John) and the 'chain of revelation' of which John is a vital link. Part One also gives some general information about the Book of Revelation, and it examines Jesus' commission of John to write the Book of Revelation. Part Two of this commentary focuses on Revelation Chapters 2-3, giving an in-depth examination to each of the letters to the seven churches. Part Two gives some historical information about the churches, and it particularly examines connections between specific terms used in the letters to the churches with terms and concepts used in other passages of Scripture. I hope to give readers a firm basis for doing further research into the final book of the Bible.

I have endeavored to make this commentary as clear as possible for all Bible students. However, a grasp of the basics of biblical Greek would be helpful in using this work. (I began writing this book when I was an M.Div. student in the Biblical and Theological Studies program at the Southern Baptist Theological Seminary in Louisville, Kentucky.) I believe that readers who have not been trained in biblical Greek may still profit from this commentary due to the transliterations and translations that I provide for each Greek term that I use. Readers who have not been trained in biblical Greek may gain a sense of unknown terms' definitions from the immediate contexts in which they occur.

In seeking to produce a concise but complete commentary, I have striven to give attention to each word of the text and to focus attention on the author's main ideas presented in the text. I have prayerfully reflected on these passages, asking the Holy Spirit for guidance, and I have looked into other commentaries to learn from the wisdom of brothers who have examined Revelation before me. I present my interpretations according to the best of my understanding and do not always argue against (or even necessarily present) alternate interpretations.

It is my sincere hope that readers find this commentary to be informative, interesting, and spiritually edifying.

-Andrew J. Lindsey: Dallas, GA; December 31, 2013.

Outline of Revelation 1-3

PART ONE

INTRODUCTION
REVELATION CHAPTER 1

Chapter One

Introduction to the Book of Revelation (Rev 1:1-3)

1 [This is the]¹ Revelation from Jesus Christ that God gave him to show his servants [the things] that must happen quickly, and he made [it]² known [by] sending [it] through his angel by his servant John³ *2* who testifies the message from God—⁴ the testimony of Jesus Christ— as many [things] as he saw. *3* Blessed is the one reading and those hearing the words of prophecy, and heeding the things written in it, for the time [is]⁵ near.

---

¹ "This is" is supplied at the beginning, as the first sentence lacks a main verb. David E. Aune, *Revelation 1-5* (Dallas: Word Books, 1997), 6.

² "It" is supplied after "made" and "sending," as these verbs refer back to "the Revelation."

³ The dative form of "John" is instrumental; for more on this, see the commentary below.

⁴ καὶ is translated with a hyphen as it is epexegetical, indicating additional information concerning "the word of God."

⁵ As is often the case in Greek, a form of the verb "to be" is understood as necessary between καιρος and εγγύς, and it is therefore supplied in the translation. The addition of a

The Mediated Revelation

The first 3 verses of Revelation present a "chain of revelation," which can be represented as follows:

1. God–> 2. Jesus Christ–> 3. John–>
4. His angel/the one reading–> 5. His servants/those hearing and heeding

The Revelation from Jesus Christ. This phrase represents the first three words of Rev 1:1 in the Greek text: Ἀποκάλυψις Ἰησοῦ Χριστοῦ (*Apokalupsis Iesou Christou*).

Ἀποκάλυψις (*Apokalupsis*) is translated "apocalypse" or "revelation." This word "expresses the subject and nature of the book,"[6] and it provides the traditional title for the book. Ἀποκάλυψις (*Apokalupsis*), or some form of this word, occurs in the New Testament "44 times (verb, 26; noun 18), nearly always with the basic thrust 'to uncover what has formerly been hidden.'"[7] "The book is a heightened form of prophecy, which can be referred to as 'apocalyptic,' as apparent from the

form of the verb "to be" will most likely remain unnoted in some of the following translation.

[6] G.K. Beale, *The Book of Revelation* (Grand Rapids: Wm. B. Eerdmans Publishing Co., 1999), 181.

[7] Grant Osborne, *Revelation* (Grand Rapids: Baker Book House, 2002), 52.

use of 'apocalypse' and 'prophecy' in vv. 1-3 and in 22:7."[8] As used in Revelation, "apocalypse" does not seem to refer to a technical genre of Greek literature, as this word for revelation and related words have specific meanings– meanings that do not necessarily coincide with extra-biblical uses of the term– both in this book and in the rest of the NT canon. Therefore, the conventions of extra-biblical "apocalyptic literature" have limited value (at best) in exegesis of the book of Revelation.

Ἰησοῦ Χριστοῦ (*Iēsou Christou*) is usually rendered "*of* Jesus Christ" in the translations and is taken by many preachers to indicate that the revelation of the book is "*concerning* Jesus Christ." Indeed, it is certain that Revelation is a Christ-centered book from John's initial vision of Jesus in chapter 1 to the Christ-directed praise uttered by the heavenly hosts in chapter 5 to the benediction at the end of chapter 22– and at all points in between– Jesus is glorified.

Currently, however, here is a wide-ranging consensus of commentators– including David Aune, Greg Beale, Grant Osborne, and Robert Thomas– who note that, as it is used in Revelation 1:1, Ἰησοῦ Χριστοῦ (*Iēsou Christou*) appears intended as a subjective genitive, so that the phrase should be rendered "*from* Jesus Christ." An understanding of the phrase as indicating Jesus

---

8   Beale, *The Book of Revelation*, 181.

Christ as the chief agent of the revelation related by John, rather than as the content of the revelation related by John, fits better within verse 1, in which the content of the revelation seems to be "[the things] that must happen quickly." As noted above, "revelation" indicates an uncovering of "what has formerly been hidden." If this understanding of verse 1 is correct, then John is indicating that Jesus Christ is *uncovering* "[the things] that must happen quickly." This understanding would also make sense of why the book is referred to as "the words of prophecy" in 1:4, and would fit well with the Christology presented in John's Gospel in which Jesus is called the "Word," and is seen as God's chief agent of special revelation (John 1:1, 18).

The Revelation given to Jesus Christ by God. ἣν ἔδωκεν ᾽αυτῷ ᾽ο θεὸς δεῖξαι τοῖς δούλοις ᾽αυτους ἃ δεῖ γενέσθαι ᾽εν τάχει (*hēn edōken autō ho theos deixai tois doulois autous ha dei genesthai en tachei*) is translated "that God gave him to show his servants [the things] that must happen quickly."

᾽ο θεὸς (*ho theos*) is, as usual, translated, "God." In Revelation 1:1 "God" is clearly meant to signify "God the Father:" the first Person of the Trinity. Referring to "God the Father" simply as "God" is common in the NT. Jesus is often referred to as "the Son of God," and "God" in this phrase is not meant to refer to God in His essential unity (so that "the Son of God" would nonsensically make Jesus His own Son!), but to the Person known as "God the Father of our Lord Jesus Christ" (Col 1:3). There are a great number of verses that speak of "God" and "Jesus" as distinct Persons (see, for example, Jesus' words in John 17:3) without taking anything away from the Deity of Christ.

Though essentially One, the three Persons of the Trinity are revealed to take on distinct roles, so that (for example) the Father sent the Son into the world (John 8:42), and not vice-versa, and it was the Son, not the Father, who suffered and died upon the Cross.

Likewise, God the Father is demonstrated as the Person of the Godhead who is the distinct Author of revelation. In the first chapter of John's Gospel, God [the Father] is distinct from the Word (though, mysteriously, One with the Word as well: John 1:1), and it is the Word who reveals God (John 1:18). Similarly, in Hebrews 1:1-2 God [the Father] is the One speaking, and the Son is the One through whom He speaks. In Revelation 1:1 God is the Author of revelation, while Jesus Christ is the unique Agent of revelation from whom the revelation comes to the other members of the 'chain' outlined above.

As the reader will begin to perceive, it is impossible to truly contemplate God without contemplating His Word–Jesus Christ–and so the thought of God the Father as the distinct Author of revelation may become more intelligible as the reader focuses on Jesus Christ: the unique Agent of revelation.

ʼαυτῷ (*autō*), the word translated "him," must refer to "Jesus Christ," the only "him" (other than God the Father) mentioned in the text thus far. As indicated above, the text asserts that God gave Jesus the Revelation. Knowledge of God, who is spirit (John 4:24), is always mediated to His creation by His Word: from creation in Genesis 1 to the call of Abram in Genesis 12, from the vision of the valley of dry bones in Ezekiel 37 to the coming of the Word in flesh, God has always been known by His Word. The NT identification of Jesus Christ as the "Word," who is *with* God and who *is* God (John 1:1) is fundamental to a right understanding of who God is. That our knowledge of God is a mediated knowledge is one reason why it is so important for us to acknowledge and proclaim that there is "one Mediator between God and Man" (1 Tim 2:5b): that is, Christ Jesus, who is both fully God and fully Man.

In Revelation 1:1, God gives the "revelation"– the "words of prophecy" (v. 3)– to Jesus Christ, His primary agent of revelation, in order "to show His servants [the things] that must happen quickly." What the author makes explicit in Revelation 1:1– God giving revelation to Jesus Christ for the benefit

of His servants– is not an unusual process, but it is
how God has always revealed spiritual truth.

The Revelation through His angel. καὶ
'εσήμανεν 'αποστείλας διὰ τοῦ 'αγγέλου 'αυτοῦ
(*kai esēmanen aposteilas dia tou angelou autou*) is
translated "and he made [it] known [by] sending [it]
through his angel." The "angel" here is a messenger.
"Angel" is used somewhat figuratively. "His angel"
in Rev 1:1 is identified with "the one reading"
in Rev 1:3, as explored below. According to the
understanding that I propose, "angel" is singular
here because– in accordance with Rev 1:20– each
church would have had a single "angel" responsible
for sending or declaring the message from Jesus
Christ by John to that church.

The Revelation to His servant John. τῷ
δούλῳ 'αυτοῦ 'Ιωάννῃ (*tō doulō autou Iōannē*) is
translated "by his servant John." Other translations
render the dative form of John in Rev 1:1 simply
according to its function as an indirect object: "to
John." This translation would give the impression
that the Book of Revelation is transmitted from
Jesus Christ through His angel *to* John:

Jesus Christ-> His angel -> John.

This translation/understanding is certainly a
possibility, at least in terms of the paragraph in
which the phrase occurs. John writes in Revelation

10:9 and 17:1ff. that particular angels spoke to him, and John overhears angels (and other heavenly beings) speaking throughout the book. Understanding the phrase in Revelation 1:1 τῷ δούλῳ ἀυτοῦ Ἰωάννῃ (*tō doulō autou Iōannē*) as the indirect object "*to* his servant John"– along with a consideration of Rev 22:6,8,16– would indicate that [virtually] everything that John saw and heard was revealed to him by a specific angel.

Furthermore, though the risen Christ certainly spoke directly to His apostles (as He did to John in Revelation 1-3 or to Saul in Acts 9:4-6; 26:14-18, calling Saul to be an apostle), God often delights in honoring His created servants by employing them to minister to others. This general principle is especially true in God's giving of Scripture. So even when it is not clear that a specific passage was given through angels, it may be the case that they were often employed: as seen when Paul in Galatians 3:19 writes that the Law was given through angels. When reading the Law, is not obvious that angels administered it (the reader may think that God gave it directly to Moses), but in Gal 3:19 the Holy Spirit reveals a 'chain of revelation' for the Law:

1. YHWH–> 2. angels–> 3. "an intermediary"/ Moses–> 4. the people of Israel

However, I have translated τῷ δούλῳ ᾿αυτοῦ ᾿Ιωάννῃ (*tō doulō autou Iōannē*) according to the instrumental use of the dative: "*by* his servant John." According to this understanding, the revelation is transmitted from Jesus Christ *by* John through His angel:

Jesus Christ–> John –> His angel.

Most translators, it seems, cannot imagine that John would be an intermediary between Jesus Christ and His angel (rather than His angel being an intermediary between Jesus Christ and John), but this is exactly what we see starting in Chapter 2, in which Jesus Christ commands John to write to "the angel" of the various churches. This will be further explored in the comment on Rev 1:20 below.

John is simply called "his servant" in Revelation 1:1; "his" refers to "Jesus Christ's" as in Jude 1, rather than to "God [the Father]'s:" in other words, this verse *seems* to be calling John the "servant of [the Person] Jesus Christ" *rather than* the "servant of [the Person] God [the Father]." The term is rather ambiguous, however, and this is no surprise as:

1. The revelation comes *from* God [the Father] *through* Jesus Christ;
2. NT authors variously refer to themselves as "servant[s] of Jesus Christ" (as in Jude 1 or Romans 1:1) or "servant[s] of God *and* of the Lord Jesus Christ" (as in James 1:1);
3. The author of Revelation clearly understands Jesus Christ to be divine and, though a distinct Person, essentially One with the Father.

John is certainly an apostle (at least in the broad sense), for he is personally commissioned for a specific ministry by the risen Christ. John also specifically refers to the book of Revelation as "words of prophecy" in Rev 1:3 and 22:7, thus signifying that he is a prophet.

Though John does not explicitly identify himself in Rev 1:1 as one of the Twelve (i.e., John the brother of James, the son of Zebedee), there are reasons to believe that the author of Revelation is the same Apostle who authored the Gospel according to John and the three epistles of John:

1. G.K. Beale notes several themes (such as Exodus-Moses motif, Jesus as Word, Lamb, and Son of man and as glorified even through death, etc.) and some words and phrases common to Revelation, the Gospel

according to John, and the three epistles of John.

2. *The Apologetics Study Bible* notes facts of the historical situation: that the writer of Revelation had personal relationships with the churches of Asia Minor, as the Apostle John was known to have; the circumstances of the author of Revelation match the known circumstances of the Apostle John.

3. Furthermore, there is no "John" other than the Apostle John who is known to have had such prominence as to refer to himself simply as "John" and have his identity known to the churches.

4. John MacArthur notes that several early Church witnesses, such as Justin Martyr, Irenaeus, Clement of Alexandria, and Tertullian, identified the Apostle John as the author of Revelation.

John forms a vital link in the 'chain of revelation.' Without this man– this apostle and prophet– those on the other side of the equation ("His angel/the one reading" and "His servants/those hearing") have nothing to read nor hear, and thus no connection with what God has revealed. We in the Church– "God's household," which is built on the foundation of the apostles and prophets (Eph. 2:19-20)– are in the same position as the original reader and hearers of the Book of Revelation; we have access to what God has revealed only through the written record given to us through the prophets and apostles. In our hyper-egalitarian society this is hard to hear: we believe that we should all have equal access to every possible experience with God, but God has elevated the NT apostles to a special position, and we are dependent on their teachings if we are to know Him rightly. The reason that we have the NT is because the Christians in the first century honored the writings of the apostles– they did not expect that they would each be visited by the risen Jesus before His Second Coming and receive words directly from Him– they cherished, memorized, studied and preserved the words they were given. We, similarly, in seeking a personal relationship with God, should not cut ourselves off from the means that God has given for establishing that relationship by neglecting the words of the prophets and apostles.

The Role of His Servant John

John's role in Revelation is to bear witness or testify concerning "the message of God– the testimony of Jesus Christ." As in John's Gospel account (John 19:35; 21:24), and as in John's first epistle (1 John 1:1), in Revelation, John sees himself primarily as an eyewitness to an historical event.

John encounters the glorified Christ in a specific location on a specific day (Rev 1:9-10) and receives a specific word from Him, which he is charged with delivering. That John is providing eyewitness testimony is further indicated by the last phrase in Revelation 1:2, ὅσα εἶδεν (*hosa eiden*) "as many [things] as he saw."

John's primary testimony is concerning τὸν λόγον τοῦ θεοῦ (*ton logon tou theou*), translated above as "the message from God" to avoid confusion. This phrase is often translated "the Word of God;" in this case, however, the phrase is not (at least primarily) intended to indicate "the Word of God" as Christians usually understand it today (i.e., "the Bible" in general). Rather, in keeping with the introductory nature of these verses, τοῦ θεου (*tou theou*) should be taken as a phrase in the subjective category of the genitive case. In other words, this is a "word" or "message" *from* God. Again, as Robert L. Thomas notes: in keeping with the introductory character of the opening verses of this book, τὸν λόγον τοῦ θεοῦ (*ton logon tou theou*), "the message of God" is a "further characterization of the contents of [Revelation]... [this phrase] is the common idiomatic phrase for a direct prophetic communication, exactly what this book purports to be."[9]

---

[9] Robert L. Thomas, *Revelation 1-7* (Chicago: Moody Press, 1992), 59.

The specific "message of God" about which John testifies in Revelation is further defined as τὴν μαρτυριάν Ἰησοῦ Χριστοῦ (*tēn marturian Iēsou Christou*) "the testimony of Jesus Christ."[10] Unlike in the first verse of Revelation, Ἰησοῦ Χριστου (*Iēsou Christou*) in Rev 1:2 *does* mean "concerning Jesus Christ;" John's primary communication to the churches is a message from God consisting of a testimony about the glorified Christ, as he begins to describe in the following verses.

A Beatitude

μακάριος (*makarios*): this blessing begins a verse that is the culmination to the introduction of the book, linking the revelation from Jesus through the angels testified by John to the churches of Asia Minor, and offering a special measure of happiness to the one reading and heeding, and those hearing and heeding, the words of prophecy.[11]

Before considering those to whom the blessing in Rev 1:3 is addressed, it is important to note the phrase τοὺς λόγους τῆς προφητείας (*tous logous tēs prophēteias*), which is translated "the words of prophesy." This phrase is seen as key

---

[10]   The καὶ is taken as epexegetical.

[11]   Evans points out that "blessed" in the Bible means "to experience, enjoy, and extend [to others] the favor of God in your life." Tony Evans, *Between a Rock and a Hard Place* (Chicago: Moody Publishers, 2010), 99.

in determining the literary genre of the book. Whether or not the book can be understood to fit into the category of apocalyptic literature (and to what degree), the author of the work obviously understands Revelation to be primarily a book of prophecy. τῆς προφητείας (*tēs prophēteias*) is to be understood as a genitive of apposition so that this phrase is referring to the same concept as the preceeding τοὺς λόγους (*tous logous*). The idea, then, is that τοὺς λόγους τῆς προφητείας (*tous logous tēs prophēteias*) means "the words which constitute this prophecy."[12] This phrase further highlights the author's claim that he is delivering a divine message.

It is also important to note the urgency that makes this blessing necessary. The one reading and heeding, and those hearing and heeding, "the words of prophecy" need a special blessing because "the time [is] near." The "time" indicated in this verse does not necessarily refer to the Second Coming of Christ, but (more probably) to the time of trials discussed in the following verses.

To the one reading and heeding. Though the blessing mentioned above may be applied to the individual reader, the primary intention seems to refer to one publicly reading the "words of prophecy" within the context of a local church of Christians. Pastors were expected to publicly

---

[12] Aune, *Revelation 1-5*, 7.

read Scripture (see 1 Tim 4:13) and John would similarly expect pastors of the churches receiving his "words of prophecy"– the divine message "from Jesus Christ"– to read the Revelation to their churches. As explored below, "the one reading and heeding" in Revelation 1:3 is identified with "His angel" from Rev 1:1 and the "angel" of each church, beginning in Rev 1:20.

To those hearing and heeding. The original audience for Revelation would have had a lower literacy rate than that enjoyed by our current society. Furthermore, there would have been very few copies of Revelation until many years after John penned this book. Therefore, the main way that Christians would encounter Revelation is through hearing it read aloud when meeting together.

τηροῦντες (*terountes*) is translated "heeding." This participle is properly understood as applied to both "the one reading" and "those hearing." Someone could be within earshot of someone reading these verses aloud– someone could even be the actual reader– and yet miss the blessing indicated in this verse. It is not the one who merely *reads* or *hears* Revelation who is "blessed," but it is the one who reads/hears and *heeds*–listening attentively to put the words into practice, upon whom the 'chain of relation' (mentioned above) terminates. It is the person who *heeds* who receives the promised blessing of Rev 1:3.

Chapter Two

Introduction of the Epistle to the Seven Churches (Rev 1:4-8)

4 John,

To the seven churches in Asia:Grace to you[13] and peace from He[14] who is and was and is coming, and from the sevenfold Spirit[15] who is before his throne, **5** and from Jesus Christ, the faithful witness, the firstborn from the dead and the ruler of the kingdoms of the earth.

To him [who][16] loves us and released us from our sins by his blood, **6** and

---

[13] This is the second person plural [i.e., "y'all"], rather than the second person singular.

[14] ὁ is the nominative masculine singular definite article and so is translated "he." The phrase ὁ ὤν καὶ ὁ ἦν καὶ ὁ ἐρχόμενος is taken as a circumlocution, used as an indeclinable divine name. ὁ is translated only at the head of the clause, as each occurrence refers to the same "He."

[15] See the following commentary regarding this verse for an explanation of why τῶν ἑπτὰ πνευμάτων is translated "the sevenfold Spirit."

[16] "Who" is supplied because the phrase in which it occurs is literally rendered "the [dative masculine singular] loving us." The dative, in this case, is the indirect object the subject being the letter that John was in the process of writing.

made us a kingdom, priests to his God
and Father: to him [be] the glory and the
power forever.

    –Amen.

7 Behold, he is coming with the clouds,
and every eye will see him,
and whoever pierced him,
and all the tribes of the earth
will anguish[17] over him.

    –It is certain.[18]

8 "I am the Alpha and the Omega,"[19] says
the Lord God, "He who is and was and is
coming, the Almighty."

---

[17] κόψονται has been traditionally rendered "mourn;" after much prayer, study, and consideration, I have opted to translate this term as "anguish," as the 'mourning' here does not seem to refer to the grief over losing a loved one (which is the sole context in which most modern readers would understand the word "mourn"), but rather it refers to a deeply painful sorrow over personal guilt.

[18] ναί, ἀμήν is a synonymia, "whose function is to strengthen the certainty of what has just been prophesied." Thomas, *Revelation 1-7*, 79.

[19] There is no theological significance to the fact that the word for "Alpha" is spelled out in the Greek text, while "Omega" is given as a single letter; that is, the phrase τὸ Ἄλφα καί τὸ Ω (*to Alpha kai to Ō*) appears uneven in the Greek text, but this is simply because Greek grammarians did not coin the word Ὤμεγα until the 7th century A.D. (Aune, *Revelation 1-5*, 57.)
"The Alpha and the Omega" could reasonably be translated as "the A and the Z" so that the one reading in English could immediately see that the Lord God is using the first and last

Salutation and Blessing from God Through John

χάρις ὑμῖν καὶ ἐιρήνη (*charis humin kai eirēnē*): "grace to you and peace." In Revelation 1:4 John uses a greeting that is identical to that normally used by the Apostle Paul at the beginning of his letters to the churches (see Rom 1:7, 1 Cor 1:3, 2 Cor 1:2, Gal 1:3, Eph 1:2, Phil 1:2, Col 1:2, 1 Thess 1:1, 2 Thess 1:2), a form of which is also used by the Apostle Peter in his letters (see 1 Pet 1:2, 2 Pet 1:2), similar to the greeting John used in his second epistle (see 2 John 1:3). John thus connects Revelation with the authoritative letters of the apostles to the churches: the then-emerging NT canon. This common greeting of "grace to you and peace" is adapted from the blessing that the LORD told His servant Moses to speak to Aaron, that Aaron and his sons might bless the children of Israel (see Num 6:22-26).[20] This greeting expresses the desire of the author that his readers experience God's favor and safety in Him. As it is expressed in the NT, this greeting is a proof for the deity of Christ,

---

letter of the alphabet. The traditional anglicized forms of the Greek letter names– "Alpha and Omega"– is retained because the phrase "the A and the Z" is not commonly used in English and rendering reading "the A and the Z" may have an unintended comic effect.

[20] Notice the 'chain of revelation' from this passage in Numbers.

since the blessing from the LORD in Numbers 6 is now often extended in the name of both God [the Father] and Jesus Christ. As mentioned below, the particular form of the greeting in Rev 1:4-5a gives a very strong hint of the Trinity.

ὁ ὤν (*ho ōn*) "He who is" is a name for God used among Greek-speaking Jews, following the LXX translation of Exodus 3:14. Aune notes that, "Just as Moses was told by God to accredit his message by telling the people that ὁ ὤν had sent him, so John appears to be authenticating his prophetic book by claiming that its actual source is none other than ὁ ὤν."[21] Furthermore, τῶν ἑπτὰ πνευμάτων (*tōn epta pneumatōn*) is understood in Rev 1:4 to indicate "the sevenfold Spirit," taken as a way of representing the Holy Spirit in His fullness. This language concerning the Holy Spirit originated in the LXX version of Isaiah 11:2-3 and Zechariah 4:2,10. (Additionally, the Spirit is here spoken of as being "seven" or "sevenfold" due to the fact that He ministers to the seven churches of Asia.[22]) Therefore, in Rev 1:4-5, we have a greeting

---

[21] Aune, *Revelation 1-5*, 31.

[22] Osborne, *Revelation*, 61. Schreiner points out that the fact the first number in the Book of Revelation is clearly figurative should alert readers that subsequent numbers are also figurative. Thomas Schreiner, "Grace from the Father, Son, and Spirit," Revelation 1:1-8 (sermon, *Clifton Baptist Church*, 14 September 2008); accessed 14 January 2014; available from http://cliftonbaptist.org/sermons-and-audio/; Internet.

that echoes a blessing from the LORD in the OT: a blessing that is now extended in the name of God [the Father], the Holy Spirit, and Jesus Christ.

In Revelation 1:5 Jesus Christ is named (among other titles) as ὁ μάρτυς ὁ πιστός (*ho martus ho pistos*) "the faithful witness," further pointing to Christ as the chief agent of revelation.[23] Jesus is furthermore named ὁ πρωτόκος τῶν νεκρῶν (*ho prōtokos tōn nekrōn*) "the firstborn from the dead." This phrase seems to be a title for Christ that was common in the early Christian community. This phrase is previously recorded in Colossians 1:18. In that context, this phrase is part of what seems to be an early Christian hymn, incorporated into the letter. The epistle of Colossians was circulated in the Roman province of Asia, including Laodicea (Col 4:16), so the original readers of Revelation may have already been familiar with this title for Christ.[24] ὁ πρωτόκος τῶν νεκρῶν (*ho prōtokos tōn nekrōn*) "the firstborn from the dead" naturally captures readers' attention as it is a literary paradox.

Having been raised from the dead, Jesus is now and will further be manifested as ὁ ἄρχων τῶν βασιλέων τῆς γῆς (*ho archōn tōn basileōn tēs gēs*) "the ruler of the kingdoms of the earth." Though in the days of Revelation various rulers

---

[23] See the discussion in Chapter 1 above.

[24] Aune, *Revelation 1-5*, 38.

were oppressing the churches (and intense state-sponsored persecution happens in many places even today), the Lord of the Church is actually the sovereign over all nations. This is revealed more fully in Revelation 19:19 as various "kings of the earth" are gathered together in rebellion to make war against the glorified One who is named the "Word of God," "the King of Kings and Lord of Lords" (Rev 19:13, 16); these "kings of the earth" suffer immediate and decisive defeat (Rev 19:20-21).

Dedication of the Epistle to Jesus Christ

John dedicates his writing to Jesus Christ in Rev 1:5b, praising Him as the One who has glory and power forever. In his dedication of this writing to Jesus Christ, John highlights three specific ways in which Jesus blesses believers: *He loves us, He released us* from our sins by His blood, and *He made us* something different than we were before: a kingdom, priests to His God and Father.[25]

This last phrase– βασιλείαν, ἱερεῖς (*basileian, hiereis*) "a kingdom, priests"– is based on a similar phrase in Exodus 19:6 (βασιλείαν, ἱεράτευμα; cf.

---

[25] Notice that John tends to use aspects of the Revelation in groups of three, perhaps patterned on the revelation of "[God]... "the sevenfold Spirit"... and "Jesus Christ" (Rev 1:4-5).

MT).[26] Though some have translated this phrase, "a kingdom of priests," Aune notes, "when Rev. 1:6 is compared with 5:10 (where the phrase βασιλείαν καὶ ἱερεῖς, 'kingdom and priests,' is found, also alluding to Exodus 19:6), [it is clear that] John is thinking in terms of two privileges of the people of God rather than just one."[27] Thomas adds:

> Corporately, they are a 'kingdom,' but individually they are 'priests.' The priestly office established by the OT law was hereditary, and only members of Aaron's family were eligible. Jesus Christ has established a new family relationship by which all believers have a priestly ministry to God.[28]

A Prophecy of Jesus Christ's Coming

Having referred to his writing as "the words of prophecy" in verse 3, John now prophesies to his readers.

The prophecy. Ἰδοὺ (*idou*) translated, "Behold!" is characteristic in the book of Revelation as indicative of special divine intervention and should be understood in this case as introducing

---

[26] Beale, *The Book of Revelation*, 193.

[27] Aune, *Revelation 1-5*, 47.

[28] Thomas, *Revelation 1-7*, 71.

an oracle or prophecy. Ἰδοὺ has two related meanings: (1) "It functions as a marker of strong emphasis indicating the validation of the statement it introduces;" (2) "It functions as a marker to draw attention to that which it introduces."[29]

The prophecy in Revelation 1:7 draws upon Daniel 7:13 and Zechariah 12:10: texts Jesus used to prophesy of His coming in judgment, as recorded in Matthew 24:30. Citing Acts 2:22-23, 36; 7:52 (among other texts) and connecting Rev 1:7 to Jesus' prophecy in Matt 24, Gentry plausibly argues that "whoever pierced him" refers to the Jews who actually called for Jesus' crucifixion. This argument is strengthened when one considers that Zechariah 12 seems to be firmly centered upon Jerusalem, and that "tribes" in Rev 1:7 would have likely carried a Jewish connotation to the original readers (as per the twelve tribes of Israel).[30]

Assurance the message will come to pass. The One from whom John had received the prophecy recorded in verse 7 announces Himself in verse 8. This declaration from the Lord God highlights His sovereignty over the course of history and thus serves as an assurance that the prophecy will come to pass.

---

[29] Aune, *Revelation 1-5*, 53.

[30] K.L. Gentry, *Before Jerusalem Fell* (Tyler: Institute for Christian Economics, 1989), 123-131.

In Revelation 1:8, the Lord God first refers to Himself as τὸ Ἄλφα καὶ τὸ Ω (*to Alpha kai to Ō*) "the Alpha and the Omega." This divine title emphasizes the sovereignty of God in a way similar to the titles "the beginning and the end" (Rev 21:6; 22:13) and "the first and the last" (Rev 1:17; 2:8; 22:13).[31]

The Lord God next refers to Himself as ὁ ὢν καὶ ὁ ἦν καὶ ὁ ἐρχόμενος (*ho ōn kai ho ēn kai ho erchomenos*), "He who is and was and is coming." This phrase is repeated from verse 4. In the former verse, this phrase clearly referred to God the Father as the phrase occurred in the first section of a Trinitarian formula. In this verse, the reader may ask if the phrase is once again in reference to the Father, or if it is now specifically applied to the Son. But the Trinitarian distinction made a few verses earlier does not seem to be in view with this verse; rather, God in the fullness of His divine essence is being magnified. That this verse *takes in* a reference to the Son in His deity along with the Father is seen in that: (1) "He who... is coming" in this context most naturally includes the idea of the One who is said to be "coming" in the previous verse– that is, the One who was also said to be "pierced"– namely, Jesus; (2) ὁ ὢν (*ho ōn*) "He who is" is basically the third person form of Ἐγώ εἰμι (*Egō eimi*) "I am," and John consistently

---

31 Ibid., 57.

records Jesus referring to Himself as "I am;" (3) In Revelation 22:13, Jesus is clearly the speaker, and He refers to Himself using a title for the Lord God also found in this verse: τὸ Ἄλφα καί τὸ Ω (*to Alpha kai to Ō*) "the Alpha and the Omega."

The final title by which the Lord God refers to Himself in this verse is ὁ παντοκράτωρ (*ho pantokratōr*) "the Almighty." This divine title occurs eight other times in the book of Revelation (4:8; 11:17; 15:3; 16:7, 14; 19:6, 15; 21:22).[32] In Revelation 1:8, "the Almighty" summarizes the two previous phrases by which the Lord God identifies Himself– phrases that were rather poetic– into a single term. The Lord God can and will bring His prophecy to pass because He is "the Almighty:" the one who controls all things.

---

[32] There is only one other verse in the NT in which the term "the Almighty" is used– 2 Corinthians 6:18– and this is an OT quotation. (Thomas, *Revelation 1-7*, 81)

Chapter Three

Commission of John to Write the Book of Revelation (Rev 1:9-20)

9 I, John– your[33] brother and co-fellowshipper in the hardship and kingdom and perseverance in Jesus– came to be on the island called Patmos due to the message of God and the testimony of Jesus. **10** I was in [the] Spirit on the Lord's Day when behind me I heard a loud voice like a trumpet **11** saying, "Write[34] what you see into a book and send it to the seven churches: to Ephesus,[35] Smyrna, Pergamum, Thyatira, Sardis, Philadelphia, and Laodicea."

12 And I turned to see the voice of whoever was speaking with me; and,

---

[33] This is the second person plural possessive [i.e., "y'all's"], rather than the second person singular.

[34] The imperative "write" is brought to the forefront of this verse to convey the point that this verse is a command.

[35] Greek tends to separate all items in a list with a conjunction, whereas English uses commas to separate items in a list, only using a conjunction before the final item; therefore, many instances of και will be left untranslated except by punctuation.

having turned, I saw seven golden lamp-stands, **13** and in [the] middle of the lamp-stands [one] like a son of man having been clothed in a long flowing robe reaching down to [his] feet, and having been girded around the chest with a golden sash. **14** His head– that is, his hair– [was] white like wool– white as snow– and his eyes [were] like flames of fire. **15** And his feet resembled fine bronze as fired in a furnace, and his voice [was] like the sound of many waters. **16** And [he was][36] holding seven stars in his right hand, and a sharp, two-edged sword was going forth from his mouth, and his appearance [was] like the sun, shining in power.

17 And when I saw him, I fell before his feet like a dead man,[37] and he placed his right hand on me, saying, "Don't be afraid! I am the First and the Last, **18** the Living One, and I was dead– *but behold!*–

---

[36] A form of εστιν (rendered "he was" in translation) must have been understood by the original audience to be supplied in the readers' thinking between και and ἔχων. This understood εστιν would have been the controlling verb for this verse, yielding "was" in the translation again after "appearance" (ὄψις).

[37] νεκρος, being NMS and anarthrous, is translated "a dead man."

I am living from forever into forever, and
I hold the keys to death and to Hades.[38]
19 Therefore, write down the things that
you saw, and the things that are, and the
things that are about to happen. **20** [As
for][39] the mystery of the seven stars that
you saw in my right hand and the seven
golden lamp-stands: the seven stars are
the angels of the seven churches and
the seven lamp-stands are the seven
churches.

Context of the Commission

John wrote Revelation from the island of Patmos,
having been exiled there due to his testimony for
Christ. Of Patmos, Aune notes: "Patmos (now
Patino), one of the Sponades Islands, is thirty
miles or forty-five kilometers in circumference
and is located thirty-seven miles west-southwest
from Miletus, fifty miles from ancient Ephesus."[40]

---

[38] Καὶ is translated in different ways based on the context.
The first καὶ is understood as epexegetical. Rather than
forming the third part of a description [the First and the Last
and the Living One], this should be understood as a further
insight into the previous description of Christ's eternality
[the First and the Last, *even* the Living One].

[39] In regard to this "as for," see the comment below on το
μυστηριον.

[40] Aune, *Revelation 1-5*, 76-77.

Thomas adds: "It was the last stopping place when traveling from Rome to Ephesus and the first stopping place on a return trip to Rome."[41] This geographical connection with Ephesus most likely explains why Ephesus is mentioned first in the list of "the seven churches."

John, writing to churches that are experiencing various degrees of difficulty or persecution, is himself no stranger to suffering for Christ. Rather (as demonstrated by his then-current unjust exile), he is their "co-fellowshipper" in "hardship." But this "hardship" is not alone; the present experience of hardship is a means used by God to bring His disciples into the full experience of His kingdom. Notice the striking similarity of the language used in Rev 1:9 and in Acts 14:22, in which it is declared that "[it is] through many hardships that we must enter into the kingdom of God." The "hardships" faced by followers of Jesus occur for a purpose, and this purpose will certainly be fulfilled, which is why John encourages his readers with the term "perseverance." Hardship, kingdom participation, and perseverance are seen as inseparably connected throughout the Book of Revelation (and in the NT as a whole), and the truth of this connection is seen in the language of Rev 1:9 as well; the terms are introduced with a single article ("*the* hardship and kingdom and perseverance," as

---

[41] Thomas, *Revelation 1-7*, 87.

facets of one experience in this earthly existence, rather than "the hardship and the kingdom and the perseverance").

In introducing his revelatory experience, John writes that he was ἐν πνεύματι (*en pneumati*) "in [the] Spirit." The "Spirit" mentioned in Rev 1:10 is certainly the Holy Spirit. Notice that the Holy Spirit was not directly mentioned in the 'chain of revelation' outlined at the beginning of Revelation. However, the early church clearly understood the Holy Spirit to be the agent of prophetic visions (see Acts 2:17; 7:55), and so the mention of "words of prophecy" in Rev 1:3 and the phrase "in [the] Spirit" here would certainly have called to mind the work of the Holy Spirit. Three other times in the Book of Revelation, John writes that he is "in the Spirit" (Rev 4:2; 17:3; 21:10); each of these times, he receives prophetic visions.[42] Moreover, John's declaration of his spiritual condition while receiving "the words of prophecy" is reminiscent of Ezekiel's repeated testimony concerning the Holy Spirit granting *him* prophecy (Eze 2:2; 3:12, 14, 24; 11:1; 43:5). In the case of John's prophecy, as with the prophet Ezekiel, the Holy Spirit replaces John's

---

[42] Thomas Schreiner, "Trusting in the Son of Man," Revelation 1:9-20 (sermon, *Clifton Baptist Church*, 21 September 2008); accessed 15 January 2014; available from http://cliftonbaptist.org/sermons-and-audio/; Internet.

normal sensory perception with a special, spiritual perception.

Though John does not mention the *year* in which he received his prophecy Rev 1:10 (scholars may wish that he had written 'in the twelfth year of Nero's reign' or 'in the first year of Caesar Domitian')[43], he does mention the *day* on which Jesus appeared to him: namely, τῇ κυριακῇ ἡμερα (*tē kuriakē hēmera*) "the Lord's Day." Referring to the first day of the week as the Lord's Day was the normal practice of the early church, as seen in a number of early Christian writings.[44] Both Acts 20:7 and 1 Corinthians 16:1-2 indicate that, from the earliest times, Christians met together on the first day of the week, that day being associated with Jesus' resurrection (Matt 28:1; Mark 16:2, 9; Luke 24:1; John 20:1, 19), the Apostle Thomas' confession of Jesus as "my Lord and my God!" (John 20:26), and Jesus' pouring out the Spirit at Pentecost (Lev 23:15-16; Acts 2:1-4, 32-33). Now, on the day that he is apparently used to setting aside for special worship of his resurrected Lord, John receives the ultimate canonical revelation from

---

[43] On the other hand, see Gentry's argument that Rev 17:10 is intended to identify Revelation as written in the time of Nero, the seventh "king," counting from Julius Caesar. Gentry, *Before Jerusalem Fell*, 158-159.

[44] For example, *Didache* 14:1; *Ad. Magn.* 9:1. Compare *Barnabas* 15:9; Justin Martyr, *First Apology*, Chapter 67; Tertullian, *To The Nations*, Chapter 13.

Jesus. The timing of Revelation would have made an immediate connection between the author of the book and the members of the "seven churches," who would have most likely been meeting together on the Lord's Day when they first heard the book read aloud.

The Command to Write the Book of Revelation

καὶ ἤκουσα ᾿οπίσω μου φωνὴν μεγάλην ῾ως σάλπιγγος λεγούσης, ῾Ο βλέπεις γράψον εἰς βιβλίον καὶ πέμψον ταῖς ἑπτὰ ἐκκλησίαις (*kai ēkousa opisō mou phōnēn megalēn hōs salpingos legousēs, Ho blepeis grapson eis biblion kai pempson tais hepta ekklēsiais*) in Revelation 1:10-11 is translated, "when behind me I heard a loud voice like a trumpet saying, 'Write what you see into a book and send it to the seven churches.'"

The voice like a trumpet. Imagine the surprise of one who thinks he is walking alone, only to hear a voice like a trumpet blast behind him! Even worshiping Jesus on the Lord's Day– even filled with the Spirit– John is yet shocked when he hears the voice of the risen Christ. By speaking to John with a voice like a trumpet– rather than in a whisper like a soft breeze– Jesus immediately captures John's undivided attention.

The command to write to the seven churches. In Revelation 1:4, John addresses the entire book of Revelation to "the seven churches in Asia." Likewise, the command in Rev 1:11 seems to refer to the entire book, not just chapters 2 and 3, in which specific words are spoken to the various churches. The churches are mentioned according the order in which a messenger traveling from Ephesus in a clockwise direction through Asia Minor would have visited them. These were not the only churches in Asia Minor at the time; Paul's epistles to the Galatians and the Colossians, for example, seem to be addressed to congregations other than those mentioned in Revelation 1-3. *Seven* churches are chosen because "seven" in biblical literature is indicative of completeness or fullness.[45] These seven particular churches are

---

[45] Beale notes, "The idea of completeness [for the number seven in the Bible] originates from the creation account in Genesis 1, where six days of creation are followed by the consummate seventh day of God's rest... Sometimes seven is both literal and figurative (e.g., in Leviticus 4-16 'sprinkling seven times' is both a literal action and a figurative representation of a complete, effective act). Other times it is purely figurative for completeness (e.g., Lev 26:18-28: God will punish Israel 'seven times' [or 'sevenfold'] if they do not repent– not seven distinct punishments but a complete chastisement)" [Beale, *The Book of Revelation*, 186]. Seven and a multiple of seven are used in the prophecy given in Dan 9:24ff. (where "seventy weeks" = "seventy sevens"), a passage pointing to the fulfillment of several spiritual realities. By the New Testament era, "seven" had become

chosen because their diversity reflects a certain gamut of experiences– both external and internal– faced by churches in a region under persecution: dealing with the unjust judgment of men in light of God's just judgment.

Some commentators would assert that the churches mentioned in Rev 1:11 (and further addressed in Rev 2-3) are intended to be indicative of successive periods of church history (the individual churches representing the overall state of the Church in seven distinct time-periods). Readers should reject this view on exegetical and observational grounds.

Exegetically, there is nothing within the text of Revelation that would indicate that readers should interpret the churches in such an allegorical manner; identifying these churches with seven church-ages is something that must be read *into* the text, rather than derived *from* the text. Furthermore, the letters to the churches in Revelation– along with the letters to other churches in the rest of the New Testament– show that from the very beginning different churches had different

---

synonymous for completeness to the extent that when Simon Peter strove to imagine the number of times he must forgive someone in order to be considered completely forgiving, he came up with "seven times" (notice that Jesus also corrects Peter using a figurative multiple of seven: "seventy times seven" Matt 18:21-22).

strengths and/or weaknesses; they were not all part of a single "Ephesian age" of church history.[46]

Observationally, readers should note that not all churches today can be regarded as a single homogenous entity. It is simply not the case that all churches are lukewarm in nature. When one considers (for example) the underground churches in China or the persecuted churches in the Middle East, the conclusion that we are currently in the "Laodicean age" seems to be influenced more by alarm over the current state of European and American culture than by a sober, holistic view of the state of the Church across the globe. Furthermore, the notion that we are now in the Laodicean age of church history seems to be influenced by *nostalgia*; it is easy to overlook the faults of churches in the previous generation and imagine that they were part of an irreproachable "Philadelphian age" while emphasizing the faults of churches in our own generation, counting them as "Laodicean."

The words written to *each* of the seven churches– not *only* to the church in Laodicea– are applicable to churches today, just as in the rest of the New Testament words originally addressed to the churches in Corinth, Galatia, Phillipi, Collosae, etc., are applicable to churches today. *Each* of the

---

[46] Steve Gregg, *Revelation: Four Views* (Nashville: Thomas Nelson Publishers, 1997), 62-63.

letters in Rev 2-3 ends with the command, "Let he who has an ear hear what the Spirit says to the churches." This indicates that the words addressed to each of the seven churches are revealed for the benefit of every church ("what the Spirit says to the *churches*"). Indeed, every Christian ("he who has an ear") is accountable to heed the words to each of the seven churches.

Certainly there may be many churches in America that suffer from Laodicean-style tepidity and pride. On the other hand, a church may find itself more in the position of the church in Pergamum (struggling with the incursion of false teachings) or the church in Ephesus (with a passion for orthodoxy but lacking evangelistic zeal). Each church and each Christian must carefully and prayerfully discern which of the admonishments or encouragements from Rev 2-3 is most applicable in a given situation.

The Vision of the Glorified Christ

How is the reader to understand the vision of the glorified Christ as related by John? In giving a certain place ("Patmos") and time ("the Lord's Day") for his vision, John seems to be once again giving a literal, eyewitness testimony as he did in his Gospel account (John 19:35; 21:24) and in his first epistle (1 John 1:1). Yet the description of

Christ in Revelation 1:12-16 is certainly connected with Jesus' self-description to each of the seven churches in Revelation 2-3 and with specific OT passages. Moreover, some aspects concerning John's vision of Christ in Rev 1:12-16 are impossible to picture in a literal manner (for example: "[he was] holding seven stars in his right hand, and a sharp, two-edged sword was going forth from his mouth"). One must take John's spiritual state into account; as he is "in [the] Spirit," John is not seeing *only* with his eyes but with his spirit as well. John's visions may be seen as *analogous* to a dream. When dreaming, the dreamer may visualize extremely unusual things; furthermore, the dreamer may *perceive* certain information about the characters and events in the dream: information that goes beyond the items actually visualized. It seems that, somewhat like Saul on the road to Damascus (Acts 9), John had an actual encounter with the risen Christ on the island of Patmos on a particular Lord's Day. Yet the Holy Spirit allowed John to perceive truth about Jesus that went beyond what John could actually see with his eyes.

The vision of the lamp-stands. John turns to face the one speaking with him. Naturally speaking, if one were to view a person standing amidst seven lamp-stands, the person and the lamp-stands would be perceived simultaneously. And if the person standing amidst the lamp-stands had an "appearance like the sun, shining in power" (so that the lamps would, presumably, be rather dim in comparison), the luminescent person would certainly capture the viewer's attention *first*. Yet, either because Christ's appearance is momentarily veiled to John or because John is relating what he saw in such a manner as to build the most dramatic tension in his readers, John first mentions the "seven golden lamp-stands." The lamp-stands in Rev 1:12-13 recall the lamp-stand with seven lamps, which was set within the tabernacle and later the temple (Exo 25:37). But, as Jim Hamilton notes: "the most important background for what John relates here about Jesus in the midst of the seven lampstands is what Zechariah saw as stated in Zechariah 4:1-14." Hamilton continues:

> Zechariah saw a lampstand with seven lamps flanked by "two olive trees" (4:2,3). Zechariah 4 presents an angel explaining the meaning of the lampstand and the two olive trees to Zechariah. John sees Jesus standing in the midst of seven lampstands, and in 1:20 Jesus interprets the meaning of the lampstands for John.
>
> The lampstand Zechariah saw points to the successful rebuilding of the temple and the renewal of God's presence among

his people (4:4-10). The two olive trees are explained as the "two anointed ones [lit., 'two sons of oil'] who stand by the Lord of the whole earth" (4:11-14). In Zechariah these two anointed ones are the anointed priest, Joshua (cf. 3:1-10), and the descendant of David, Zerubbabel (4:1-14). This text and others like it seem to have given rise to the expectation of two messiahs, one priestly and one royal, as seen in the documents found at Qumran (cf. e.g., 1QS 9:11). In Zechariah the vision means that God will accomplish his purpose in the rebuilding of the temple: "Not by might, nor by power, but by my Spirit, says the LORD of hosts" (4:6). The "two olive trees," anointed and empowered, will be the means God uses to bring this about.

This scenario now finds its fulfillment in what John sees in Revelation. The Lord is not building a temple in which to dwell but a church (cf. Matthew 16:18)! The Church is not a building but believers who are "living stones" (cf. 1 Peter 2:5). Zechariah's lampstand, which symbolized the presence of God in the temple, is fulfilled by the seven lampstands of

Revelation, which symbolizes God's presence in the seven churches to whom John writes (1:20; cf. 2:5). Zechariah's "two sons of oil," Joshua the high priest and Zerubbabel the royal descendant of David, are fulfilled in Jesus, who stands among the lampstands as God's presence in his church. Jesus himself fills the offices of High Priest and High King of Israel. The vision of the lampstand and the two olive trees in Zechariah guaranteed that God would empower the rebuilding of the temple. Similarly, John's vision of Jesus among the lampstands guarantees that God will accomplish his purpose in building the church.[47]

It is crucial to note that these connections are not incidental or superficial, but they are intentional and central to the "words of prophecy" recorded by John. With careful, inspired purpose, John uses language from Zechariah to demonstrate that the purposes of the eternal God had been pictured in the prophecies of the old covenant and that they are being fulfilled in the new covenant community: the Church indwelt by Christ.

---

[47] James M. Hamilton Jr., *Revelation* (Wheaton: Crossway, 2012), 46.

The clothing of the glorified Son of Man. In many OT verses, "son of man" is used interchangeably with "man," meaning "human being" (Num 23:19; Job 16:21; 25:6; 35:8; Psa 8:4; 80:17; 144:3; Isa 51:12; 56:2; Jer 49:18, 33; 50:40; 51:43). Throughout Ezekiel, the LORD addresses the prophet as "son of man," apparently as a means of humbling Ezekiel, causing him to identify with the mass of humanity to whom the prophecy is addressed. But the most important connections for how John uses the term "son of man" in Rev 1:13 come from the visions recorded in Daniel 7:13-14, in which one "like a son of man" is presented before the Ancient of Days and is given eternal, imperishable, and universal dominion, and in Daniel 10:14, in which one "resembling the sons of men" is an agent of God's revelation, enabling the prophet Daniel to speak. The "son of man" mentioned in Daniel had been understood as a reference to the Messiah, and it is Daniel's use of this term that forms the basis for Jesus' constant utilization of the phrase "son of man" as a name for Himself in the Gospel accounts. The glorified One whom John encounters is this same Jesus, who is seen as the fulfillment of Daniel's vision, since Jesus is the ultimate agent of God's revelation and the One through whom God's kingdom is being established on earth.

The glorified "son of man" is seen in Rev 1:13 as wearing ποδήρη (*podērē*) "a long flowing robe stretching down to [his] feet." Concerning this article of clothing, Aune notes, "The term ποδήρης occurs twelve times in the LXX and always refers to a garment worn by the high priest."[48] This garment, then, reinforces the high priestly connection mentioned in the discussion of the "seven golden lamp-stands" above.

The glorified "son of man" is also περιεζωσμένον πρὸς τοῖς μαστοῖς ζώνην χρυσᾶν (*periezōsmenon pros tois mastois zōnēn chrusan*) "girded around the chest [with] a golden sash." This article of clothing again returns readers' attention to the vision recorded in Daniel 10 (in this case, Daniel 10:5); the heavenly being who serves as God's agent of revelation in that passage is said to have been girded in gold. Later in Revelation, the angels of wrath are said to have golden sashes around their chests (Rev 15:6); similar clothing is appropriate for the glorified Jesus as He is warning churches about coming judgment.

The head of the glorified Son of Man. In contrast to the lack of biblical information concerning Jesus' physical appearance before His ascension (though readers may expect that Jesus was physically unremarkable due to the prophecy of Isa 53:2), John in Rev 1:14 gives a

---

[48] Aune, *Revelation 1-5*, 93.

head-to-foot description of the glorified Lord. What John describes (as already mentioned above) is in keeping with OT accounts of heavenly beings. Jesus' eyes are reminiscent of the heavenly visitor mentioned in Daniel 10:6, who had eyes like flaming torches. The description of Christ's eyes as flames of fire is repeated in Revelation 2:18 and 19:12. Overall, the description of Jesus in Rev 1:12-16 is particularly related to the Ancient of Days in Dan 7:9, who is also described as having hair that is white like pure wool; like the titles used for Jesus earlier in this chapter, certain characteristics of Jesus' appearance are indicative of His deity.

The feet and voice of the glorified Son of Man. Jesus' feet are said to resemble χαλκολιβάνῳ ὡς ἐν καμίνῳ πεπυρωμένης (*chalkolibanō hōs en kaminō pepurōmenēs*) "fine bronze as fired in a furnace." χαλκολιβάνῳ (*chalkolibanō*) "fine bronze," which occurs in Revelation 1:15 and 2:18, but nowhere else in extant Greek literature, seems to be a specific metallurgical term denoting high-quality bronze. The feet of the glorified Son of Man once again recall the heavenly being in Daniel 10, who is said to have [arms and] "feet like burnished bronze" (Dan 10:6).

The voice of the glorified Son of Man is also described with a term that is reminiscent of the heavenly visitor mentioned in Daniel 10:6, whose speech is said to have sounded like a great multitude. In this case, however, the closer OT parallel comes from the final section of the book of Ezekiel, in which Ezekiel hears God's voice, and "the sound of His voice [is] like the sound of many waters" (Eze 43:2); the reader is to understand that Jesus speaks forth the voice of God.

Further characteristics of the glorified Son of Man. Jesus Himself tells the significance of the "seven stars in His right hand," as discussed in the last section of this chapter. John uses equivalents of the phrase ἐκ τοῦ στόματος αὐτοῦ ῥομφαία δίστομος ὀξεῖα ἐκπορευομένη (*ek tou stomatos autou rhomphaia distomos oxeia ekporeuomenē*) "a sharp, two-edged sword was going forth from his mouth" again in Revelation 2:12,16; 19:15. The OT source for this description in Rev 1:16 is Isaiah 11:4 along with Isaiah 49:2. Both of these passages are messianic prophecies: in the first, the Spirit-empowered descendant of Jesse is said to strike the earth with a rod from His mouth; in the second, the Servant of the LORD declares that God has made His mouth to be "like a sharp sword." Various NT passages are relevant to an understanding of this description of the "sword" from Jesus' mouth as well, because they either liken the Word of God to a sword (Eph 6:17; Heb 4:12), or else predict that the returning Christ will destroy the man of lawlessness (the one seeking to oppose the kingdom of God) with the breath of His mouth (2 Thess 2:8).[49] The "sword" from Jesus' mouth is certainly intended to indicate the judgment of Christ against His enemies.

Comfort in the Person and Work of Jesus Christ

When the LORD appeared to Ezekiel in His glory for the purpose of giving him prophetic visions, Ezekiel immediately fell on his face (Eze 1:28; 3:23; 43:3; 44:4). Daniel had similar experiences when receiving prophecy from a heavenly being (Dan 10:8-10; 16-19). Likewise, when Jesus appears to John in His glory for the purpose of giving him prophetic visions, John falls "before His feet like a dead man" (Rev 1:17). Jesus does not leave John in this state, however, but He comforts His friend, first by actually touching him, then by speaking words of comfort to him.

Jesus is the First and Last, the Living One. After very practically telling the terror-stricken apostle Μὴ φοβοῦ (*Mē phobou*) "Don't fear!" the first words out of the mouth of the glorified Son of Man are ἐγώ εἰμι (*egō eimi*) "I am." This phrase occurs 48 times in the NT where it is almost always attributed to Christ or God; in Revelation this phrase is uttered exclusively by God (1:8; 21:6) and Christ (1:17; 2:23; 22:16), and it is

---

49   Thomas, *Revelation 1-7*, 104.

used to make divine predications of the speaker.[50] In this case, Christ is identified as ὁ πρῶτος καὶ ὁ ἔσχατος (*ho prōtos kai ho eschatos*) "the First and the Last;" the LORD refers to Himself by this title in Isaiah 41:4; 44:6; 48:12, and now it is applied to the glorified Son of Man.[51] ὁ ζῶν (*ho zōn*) "the Living One" is to be understood as an assertion of divine aseity; the glorified "son of man" does not need anything outside of Himself to keep Himself alive (this is further demonstrated in the following section).

Jesus has conquered death and Hades. That "the Living One" is an appropriate title for the glorified "son of man" is aptly demonstrated in the fact that He had experienced death and has proven Himself the victor over death and the realm of the dead ("Hades"). It was impossible for Him to be held under the power of death (Acts 2:24) because He is εἰς τοὺς αἰῶνας τῶν αἰώνων (*eis tous aiōnas tōu aiōnōn*), a phrase that would literally be rendered something like, "into the ages from the ages." This phrase in Rev 1:18 indicates

---

[50] Aune, *Revelation 1-5*, 100-101.

[51] Schreiner points out that the LORD's declarations that He is "the First and the Last" occur in a section of Isaiah that emphasizes there is only one God; this makes it even more striking that the Son of Man would now be called "the First and the Last." Thomas Schreiner, "Faith Unto Death," Revelation 2:8-11 (sermon, *Clifton Baptist Church*, 5 October 2008); accessed 16 January 2014; available from http://cliftonbaptist.org/sermons-and-audio/; Internet.

the eternality of Christ, and it is a straightforward assertion of His deity.

A Further Command to Write

γράψον οὖν ἅ εἶδες καὶ ἅ εἰσὶν καὶ ἅ μέλλει γενέσθαι μετὰ ταῦτα (*grapson oun ha eides kai ha eisin kai ha mellei genesthai meta tauta*) in Rev 1:19 is translated, "Therefore, write down the things that you saw, and the things that are, and the things that are about to happen."

The command to John that he will write of his visions. Unlike the apostle Paul, who was not permitted to disclose the details of the visions and revelations he had received (2 Cor 12:1-7) and unlike Daniel, who was commanded to conceal at least part of the revelation he had received (Dan 12:4), John is commanded to carefully record his revelatory visions so that he may send the record of the visions to the seven churches.

The mystery of the seven stars and seven lamp-stands. μυστήριον (*mustērion*) "mystery" only occurs in the LXX within Daniel, and Beale notes that this verse may be an allusion to Daniel 2:28-29.[52] In the Bible, the term "mystery" refers to "a truth which may not be discerned as a result of intellectual deduction or inquiry, but which may be ascertained only by direct, special revelation from

---

[52] Beale, *The Book of Revelation*, 216.

God."[53] In this case, Jesus reveals the signification of the seven stars and the seven golden lamp-stands; the lamp-stands are the seven churches, previously mentioned and further explored in the following chapters, and the "stars" are the angels of the seven churches.

How is the reader to understand the ἄγγελοι (*angeloi*) "angels" mentioned in Rev 1:20? The lexicons list "messengers" as a possible translation for ἄγγελοι (*angeloi*), and some have suggested that these "messengers" should be understood as the human "overseers," "senior pastors," or "key elders" of the seven churches.[54] Others point out that in every other NT occurrence– including throughout most of Revelation– ἄγγελοι clearly indicates "angels:" the heavenly servants of God, as seen in the various contexts. So, without further indications from the text, those originally reading the book of Revelation would almost certainly have understood ἄγγελοι to mean "angels" rather than "pastors."

On the other hand, one must note that although "angel" normally indicates a supernatural, heavenly servant of God, the biblical text also records some instances in which "angel" is used

---

[53] W.A. Criswell, *The Believer's Study Bible* (Nashville: Thomas Nelson Publishers, 1991), 1803.

[54] See, for example, John MacArthur, *The MacArthur Study Bible* (Nashville: Thomas Nelson Publishers, 2006), 1963.

figuratively of a human minister. In Galatians 4:14, Paul writes that when he preached the gospel to the Galatians he was received ὡς ἄγγελον θεοῦ (*hōs angelon theou*) "as an angel of God." In Malachi 2:7 (LXX) each priest is admonished διότι ἄγγελος κυρίου παντοκράτορός ἐστιν (*dioti angelos kuriou pantokratoros estin*) "because he is an angel of the Almighty Lord."[55] These passages show that the early Christian community may have been familiar with some instances in which– through simile or metaphor– certain human ministers of God were indeed called "angels." If Revelation 1-3 uses the term "angel" in a figurative way to indicate certain human beings, it would not be the first time that Scripture does so.

As in all areas of biblical understanding, context is key to understanding the intended meaning of ἄγγελοι. Is there anything in the context that would indicate whether these "angels" in Revelation 1-3 should be understood in the usual way– as supernatural, heavenly servants of God– or in a figurative way, as speaking of human messengers? Though understanding "angels" as supernatural, heavenly beings may seem to be

---

[55] Malachi 3:1 is also relevant in this regard: the first part of this verse speaks of one who clears the way before the Lord: one who the NT identifies as John the Baptist (Mark 1:2-4), whose ministry cleared the way for the Messiah; in Malachi 3:1 (LXX) this forerunner to the Messiah is called τὸν ἄγγελόν μου (*ton angelon mou*) "my angel."

the more natural reading of the text, notice that John is commanded to write letters to these angels and that, taking Revelation 1:11 into account, writing letters to the angels is seen as equivalent to writing letters to the individual churches that are named. Unless we imagine that supernatural, heavenly beings took John's combined letters around to the seven churches in Asia Minor and let the church members know the contents of the letters, it is far more likely that the "angel" of each church should be understood as the "messenger" of each church: "the one reading" John's writings to "those hearing" (Rev 1:3). As noted above, the pastors of the churches were expected to publicly read Scripture, therefore the "seven stars" likely indicate seven pastors who had the privilege of reading the letters to the various churches.

PART TWO

LETTERS TO THE SEVEN CHURCHES
REVELATION CHAPTERS 2-3

Chapter Four

Letter to the Church in Ephesus
(Rev 2:1-7)

1 Write to the angel of the church in Ephesus:

Thus says the one holding the seven stars in his right hand, the one walking in [the] middle of the seven golden lamp-stands:

2 I know your works– your effort and endurance–[56] that you are not able to tolerate wicked people; you tested those calling themselves apostles– *but they're not!*– and you found them to be false. *3* You have endurance, you have persevered for the sake of my name, and you have not tired out.

4 But I have this against you: you left your first love. *5* Therefore, remember from where you have fallen, and repent and do the first works. But if not, I will

---

[56] The Greek text, being originally without punctuation, often uses και where the English would more naturally use punctuation marks.

come to you and remove your lamp-stand from its place, unless you repent.

6 But you have this: you hate the works of the Nicolaitans, which I also hate.

7 Let he who has an ear hear what the Spirit says to the churches: to the victor,[57] I will give to him to eat from the tree of life, which is in the paradise of God.

Introduction of the Audience and the Author

Ephesus was a port town on a flood plain. At the time that John wrote Revelation, Ephesus was on its fourth site, the previous three having been destroyed by floods (Ephesus eventually had to move down the coast again due to erosion). The church in Ephesus during John's day was meeting in a city that was fighting to keep itself together economically and geographically, as merchants and others were looking for alternative places to conduct business. Life in Ephesus was further complicated due to the prominence of the temple of Artemis in the city. This temple was dedicated to a fertility cult, and was also a political refuge offering sanctuary to those accused of crimes.

---

[57] Forms of ὁ νικων are translated as "the victor," as suggested by the *Holman Christian Standard Bible*.

To this church, noted for its endurance through hardships, Jesus introduces Himself in Revelation 2:1 (using imagery from Rev 1:12-20) as ὁ κρατῶν τοὺς ἑπτὰ ἀστέρας ἐν τῇ δεξιᾷ αὐτοῦ, ὁ περιπατῶν ἐν μέσῳ τῶν ἑπτὰ λυχνιῶν τῶν χρυσῶν (*ho kratōn tous hepta asteras en tē dexia autou, ho peripatōn en mesō tōv hepta luchniōn tōn chrusōn*) "the one holding the seven stars in his right hand, the one walking in [the] middle of the seven golden lampstands." With this phrase, Jesus emphasizes His sovereignty over the churches. Jesus walks in the midst of the churches; He has fellowship with the churches, and He observes what happens within the churches.[58]

Commendation of the Ephesians' Works

τὸν κόπον καὶ τὴν ὑπομονήν σου (*ton kopon kai tēn hupmonēn sou*) "the effort and endurance" are descriptive of τὰ ἔργα (*ta erga*) "the works" of the Ephesian Christians.[59] "Effort" seems to denote the outward activity involved in the "works" whereas "endurance" seems to denote the inward disposition toward the "works." The combination of

---

[58] Thomas Schreiner, "Losing Our First Love," Revelation 2:1-7 (sermon, *Clifton Baptist Church*, 28 September 2008); accessed 15 January 2014; available from http://cliftonbaptist.org/sermons-and-audio/; Internet.

[59] Aune, *Revelation 1-5*, 143.

these terms leads the reader to the conclusion that the "works" of the Ephesians did not consist in a few passing good deeds. Rather, as Thomas notes: "The Ephesian church was engaged in slavish toil to the point of exhaustion and endured with lasting patience every burden it encountered."[60] "The effort and endurance" of the Ephesian church is identified in Rev 2:2 with their (commended) intolerance toward the wicked false apostles. Before the apostle Paul had departed from the Ephesian church for the last time, he warned them to keep watch against deceptive heretics and schismatics from without and within (Acts 20:29-31). Later, Paul urged Timothy to remain at Ephesus in order to instruct against false teachers (1 Tim 1:3-4). Apparently, the Ephesians had begun to diligently follow Paul and Timothy's instructions. Jesus' reference to their "works" indicates that the Ephesians had likewise taken quite seriously Paul's teaching that they had been "created in Christ Jesus unto good works" (Eph 2:10).

Condemnation of the Ephesians' Heart Condition

Despite their constant vigilance regarding doctrinal purity, the Ephesian Christians had left their first love. They followed the apostolic

---

[60] Thomas, *Revelation 1-7*, 134.

teaching but not the apostolic example. Through a comparison between this passage and the language Jesus uses in Matthew 24:12-14 (in which He speaks of the love of many being extinguished just before He speaks of the gospel being proclaimed in the whole inhabited creation), and through an exploration of the "lamp-stand" imagery in this passage [see below], Beale argues that τὴν ἀγάπην... τὴν πρώτην (*tēn agapēn... tēn prōtēn*) "the first love" in Rev 2:4 does not primarily refer to the Ephesians' love for one another, nor to their love for Christ *in general*, but to "their former zealous love for Jesus [as expressed] *by witnessing to him in the world*."[61]

Admonition to the Ephesians

If Beale's understanding of "first love" is correct, then this informs an identification of τὰ πρῶτα ἔργα (*ta prōta erga*) "the first works." Under this interpretation, "the first works" in Rev 2:5 may be understood in terms of evangelism. The Ephesians are being commanded to return to a commitment to participate in fulfilling the Great Commission, to "disciple all the ethnic groups" (Matt 28:19-20).

---

[61] Beale, *The Book of Revelation*, 230 (*emphasis in original*).

Warning to the Ephesians

Jesus warns the Ephesians that if they do not "repent and do the first works," then ἔρχομαί σοι καὶ κινήσω τὴν λυχνίαν σου ἐκ τοῦ τόπου αὐτῆς (*erchomai soi kai kinesō tēn luchnian sou ek tou topou autēs*) "I will come to you and remove your lamp-stand from its place." Since Jesus had previously declared that "the seven lamp-stands are the seven churches" His statement about removing the Ephesians' lamp-stand is essentially a threat to remove their status as a church. The lamp-stand imagery as related to the church recalls Jesus' teaching in the Gospel accounts, that His followers are the "light of the world" (Matt 5:14-16): a term that, in that context, clearly carries evangelistic import. Beale further notes:

> Israel had also been symbolized by the lamp-stand emblem (e.g., Zechariah 4), but when successive generations renounced their calling to be a light to the nations (Isa 42:6-7; 49:6), God removed them as his light-bearing people and transferred the emblem of that call to the church. That the primary meaning of lamp-stand is that of witness is confirmed from Rev 11:3-7, 10, where the "lamp-stands" refer to God's "prophetic

witnesses." Similarly, Mark 4:21 and Luke 8:16 say that a "lamp" is to be put on a "lamp-stand" to shine in order to emphasize the witnessing role of those who truly possess God's revelation (cf. also Matt 5:14-16!) in close connection to the basic formula "if anyone has ears to hear let him hear" (Mark 4:23; Luke 8:8).[62]

An examination of these relevant passages clearly supports the connection between "lamp-stands" and evangelism. This connection, in turn, lends support to the assertion that the Ephesians' "first love" and "first works" directly involved evangelism.

Additional Commendation of the Ephesians

Though Jesus condemns the Ephesians' lack of proper love, He commends them for the exercise of proper hate. In our culture, the mere suggestion that Jesus may *hate* anything might be considered scandalous, but in Rev 2:6 John records the glorified "son of man" directly asserting that He *hates* the works of the Nicolaitans.

---

[62] Ibid., 231.

A couple of explanations have been proposed regarding the origin of the term Νικολαϊτῶν (*Nikolaïtōn*) "Nicolaitans." It is possible that this name comes from the word νικάω (*nikaō*) "I conquer." In this case, the Nicolaitans were apparently claiming that they were the 'conquering ones' and were, like the false teachers confronted by the Apostle Paul (Gal 3:3; Col 2:20-23), teaching a kind of perfectionism based on good works or ascetic practices. If this view is correct, then Jesus' commendation of the Ephesians for hating the Nicolaitans' *works* is especially pointed. The connection of "Nicolaitans" with *nikaō* would provide a contrast with the use of the form of *nikaō* at the end of each letter: τῷ νικῶντι (*tō nikōnti*), translated "to the overcomer" or "to the victor." The false overcomers are contrasted with the true overcomers.

On the other hand, most Greek lexicons identify the Nicolaitans as a sect associated with Nicolaus.[63] *The NET Bible* suggests that the Nicolaus in question is one of the seven original deacons mentioned in Acts 6:5. If this connection is correct, then the Nicolaitans– claiming to derive authority from someone related to the early apostolic community– may partially be identified with the false apostles previously mentioned (Rev 2:2).

---

[63] See Friberg, Louw-Nida, Thayer, and Gingrich.

Notice that these two explanations for the term "Nicolaitans" are not necessarily mutually exclusive, since those within a biblically literate community may expect that their leader's name reflects the character of his ministry: as in the case of Jesus (meaning "YHWH saves," Matt 1:21) or Peter (meaning "rock," Matt 16:18). It may be that the Nicolaitans were, in some respects, similar to the Galatian Judaizers confronted by Paul; the Judaizers claimed a close connection with the apostles, and they over-emphasized the role of their own works (see Paul's defense in Gal 2:7-9, 15-21).

Charge to Heed the Word

With the phrase ὁ ἔχων οὖς ἀκουσάτω τί τὸ πνεῦμα λέγει ταῖς ἐκκλησίαις (*ho echōn ous akousatō ti to pneuma legei tais ekklēsiais*) "let he who has an ear hear what the Spirit says to the churches" in Rev 2:7, the Lord Jesus extends this message beyond the Ephesian congregation, so that it must properly be considered by all other churches as well. As the following promise to the victor is explicitly applied to members of all the churches, it is implied that the admonitions and warnings to the Ephesians are also to be heeded by members of the other churches.

Promise to the Victor

A great promise is contained in "what the Spirit says to the churches," namely, τῷ νικῶντι δώσω αὐτῷ φαγεῖν ἐκ τοῦ ξύλου τῆς ζωῆς, ὅ ἐστιν ἐν τῷ παραδείσῳ τοῦ θεοῦ (*tō nikōnti dōsō autō phagein ek tou xulou tēs zōēs, ho estin en tō paradeisō tou theou*) "to the victor, I will give to him to eat from the tree of life, which is in the paradise of God."

τῷ νικῶντι (*tō nikōnti*) "the victor," in this context, must be understood as indicating one who is shown to be victorious in terms of persistence in both a specific hatred and a specific love: the victor is one who hates the works of false teachers and loves Christ and His gospel.

In Revelation 2:7, as later in Rev 22:12, Jesus says that He will distribute the reward in view. This is especially significant because– as recorded in Matthew 6:4, 6, 18– Jesus had indicated that God the Father would distribute rewards to the faithful. In giving out end-time rewards, Jesus once again indicates that He Himself will be directly involved in an activity that scriptural teaching consistently reserves for deity.

The specific promised reward in this passage is φαγεῖν ἐκ τοῦ ξύλου τῆς ζωῆς, ὅ ἐστιν ἐν τῷ παραδείσῳ τοῦ θεου (*phagein ek tou xulou tēs zōēs, ho estin en tō paradeisō tou theou*) "to eat from the tree of life, which is in the paradise of God." The idea of eating from the "tree of life" offers a direct connection between this last book of the Bible and the first book of the Bible. When the LORD God banished Adam and Eve from the original garden paradise of Eden due to their sin, He did so for the explicit purpose of preventing them from eating of the "tree of life," so that they would not partake of everlasting life while in their sinful state (Gen 3:22-24). But now, to "the victor," Christ restores the blessing of life that had been lost by our original parents.

"Paradise" occurs two other places in the NT–Luke 23:43; 2 Cor 12:4– and these references, along with Rev 2:7, show that the term is used as a name "for the abode of God, a permanent home for the redeemed with Christ."[64] This "permanent home" is not– as may be suspected due to the current way that "paradise" is used– on some desert island, or some place that is far away from civilization; instead, the Greek word comes from a term used for a park built within a kingdom for the pleasure of the ruler. This more urban idea of the final dwelling place– or "tabernacle"– of God with men (Rev 21:3) is consistent with the later teaching in Revelation, wherein the "new Heaven and new Earth" (Rev 21:1) is identified as "the holy city: new Jerusalem" (Rev 21:2). The final chapter of Revelation further locates the "tree of life"– and

---

[64] Thomas, *Revelation 1-7*, 153.

thus the "paradise of God"– as existing before the "throne of God" on "either side of the river" that is made of "the water of life" (Rev 22:1-2).

Chapter Five

Letter to the Church in Smyrna
(Rev 2:8-11)

8 And write to the angel of the church in Smyrna:

Thus says the First and the Last, the [one] who became dead and he lives:
9 I know your hardships: abject poverty– *but you're rich!*– and the slander from those calling themselves Jews when they're nothing but a synagogue of Satan.[65] **10** Fear nothing that you are about to suffer. Behold! The devil is about to throw some of you into prison in order that you might be tested, and you will have hardships for ten days. Become faithful unto death, and I will give you the crown of life. **11** Let he who has an ear hear what the Spirit says to the churches: the victor will certainly not be injured by the second death.

---

[65] τοῦ Σατανᾶ could be a genitive of possession ("Satan's synagogue"), a genitive of description ("a satanic synagogue"), or a genitive of relationship.

Introduction of the Audience and the Author

In Smyrna, "the first city of Rome" in Asia Minor, which had supported Julius even before he became Caesar, emperor worship was not only widespread, but also enforced by law.[66] Christians would have found it particularly difficult to make a living in an area of enforced emperor worship,[67] and this accounts for the "abject poverty" suffered by the Smyrnean church.

The names that the glorified Christ uses of Himself in addressing the Smyrnean church in Revelation 2:8 are similar to the names that Christ had already spoken of Himself in Rev 1:17-18; the difference being that in the earlier passage Christ had said He was the "Living One," whereas here He speaks more specifically in terms of His death and resurrection. These names of Christ offer two bases of hope for the persecuted Smyrneans: 1) as explored above, "the First and the Last" is a divine title, therefore the One encouraging them is God Himself; through their hardships, the Smyrneans could be sure that Jesus is in control of "the Last" as well as "the First:" He is sovereign over time, and their end was in His hands; 2) the persecuted

---

[66] Daniel E. Hatfield, "Revelation 2:8-11" (classroom lecture notes, *22440−Greek Syntax and Exegesis*, Spring 2007).

[67] Aune, *Revelation 1-5*, 161.

Smyrneans, threatened with imprisonment and death, were being encouraged by One who Himself "became dead" but now "lives" as the Conqueror of death.

Acknowledgement of the Smyrneans' Hardships

The Smyrneans found themselves in "abject poverty," yet the risen Christ encourages them through the proclamation that they are "rich." Surely the Smyrneans were poor in terms of money, yet they were rich in terms of spiritual blessings and promised rewards in the age to come. The state of the Smyrnean church stood in stark contrast to the Laodicean church, which was wealthy in terms of money, yet spiritually impoverished (Rev 3:17).

When Revelation was written, even as today, the word "synagogue" carried a Jewish connotation. The use of "synagogue" in Rev 2:9 heightens the contrast between the claimed Judaism of those who were persecuting the Smyrnean church (i.e., the persecutors' claim to follow the God of Abraham, Isaac, and Jacob) and the reality that they had rejected God as He is revealed in Christ, thereby becoming satanic. John's use of the term "synagogue of Satan"– demonstrating that those claiming to be Jews while rejecting Christ are not part of God's people– is the other side of the coin to Paul's teaching that "to be a Jew means to be circumcised in heart, which can even apply to those who are not physically circumcised, i.e., non-Jews (Rom 2:8-3:1; cf. his figurative use of 'Israel' in Gal 6:16; cf. 1 Cor 10:18)."[68] The "slander" mentioned in this verse may refer to the Jewish community denouncing Christians before the Roman authorities. Such slander would result in Christians losing the ancient Jewish exemption from enforced Roman state worship; Christians would therefore be subject to Roman persecution.

The persecution suffered by the Smyrnean Christians is primarily defined in terms of their poverty and the slander against them.[69] Christians in the West today certainly may be slandered for our faith, and we should expect this to be the case (see, for example, Matthew 5:11). On the other hand, people in the West today generally do not expect that Christians– as a group, due merely to our profession of faith– will be any more subject to poverty than others. However, there are many places in the world today in which persecution is so severe that mere identification with Christ may mean the loss of livelihood (if not the loss of life itself). During the apostolic age, the great majority

---

[68] Ibid., 162.

[69] καὶ before τὴν πτωχείαν, in this case, is epexegetical. Thomas, *Revelation 1-7*, 162.

of Christians suffered from poverty to one degree or another (see 1 Cor 1:26; Jas 2:5).

Admonition and Encouragement to the Smyrneans

The "ten days" mentioned in Rev 2:10 may be literal, but it is likely an allusion to Daniel 1:12-15, in which it is recorded that Daniel and his friends were tested for ten days. The trial facing Daniel and his friends was one of compromise concerning idolatry, as they had been instructed to eat meat that had been sacrificed to idols. The trial facing the Smyrnean Christians was one of compromise concerning idolatry as well, as they were likely being instructed to make sacrifices to Caesar as Lord.

Faithfulness unto death is the point of this text. This is evident as one considers that "in the Roman world imprisonment was the prelude to trial and execution of sentence:" in other words– unlike in America's justice system– no one was sentenced to serve time in prison; rather, prison was a "place of temporary detention."[70] The phrase at the end of verse 10, "Become faithful unto death," makes it clear that (at least) many of the Smyrnean Christians, once in prison, would face the death penalty.

---

[70] Beale, *The Book of Revelation*, 242.

Due to their support of Caesar, Smyrna was known as the crown city. In common practice, a crown was placed on the head of the deceased. This phrase– "become faithful unto death, and I will give you the crown of life"– indicates a major theme in the book of Revelation: namely, that the Lord will reward his servants who are faithful unto death with eternal life. This is not works-righteousness, as the faithfulness is not tied to any specific activity, but rather to an attitude of trust in Christ alone and fidelity to him as Lord, which– out of love for Jesus– will not fail to confess him even unto death (Jas 1:12).[71]

Charge to Heed the Word

With the exact same words found near the end of the letter to the Ephesians, the Lord Jesus charges the Smyrneans in Rev 2:11, while also expanding the following promise to all Christians.

Promise to the Victor

"The victor" is promised freedom from being injured by "the second death." "The second death" mentioned in Rev 2:11 directly implies a first death. The first death is physical, and the second death is the sentence to the lake of fire at the final judgment

---

[71] Hatfield, "Revelation 2:8-11."

(Rev 20:14).[72] Though some of the faithful may lose their lives through persecution, they will still find eternal life and freedom from any permanent harm due to the promise of Christ.[73]

---

[72] Ibid.

[73] Jesus spoke of this same reality to His followers during His earthly ministry, as recorded in Luke 21:12-19, when He told His disciples "they will put to death [some] from among you" (Luke 21:16) followed by "yet not a hair from your head shall perish" (Luke 21:18). Schreiner, "Faith Unto Death."

Chapter Six

Letter to the Church in Pergamum (Rev 2:12-17)

12 And write to the angel of the church in Pergamum:

Thus says the One having the sharp, two-edged sword:

13 I know where you dwell, where the throne of Satan [is located],[74] and you have my name and you have not denied my Faith even in the days of Antipas my witness, my faithful one, who was killed in your presence,[75] [there] where Satan dwells. **14** But I have a few things against you. There you have those adhering to the teachings of Balaam, who was teaching Balak to place a trap before the sons of Israel: to eat meat sacrificed to idols and to fornicate. **15** Similarly, you even have

---

[74] ὅπου ὁ θρόνος τοῦ Σατανα, in context, certainly refers to locality, so "is located" is added for clarity. τοῦ Σατανα is either genitive of possession ("Satan's throne), descriptive genitive (satanic throne), or subjective genitive (where Satan is enthroned/ruling).

[75] γαρ ὑμιν, literally rendered "with, beside, or among you," is translated "in your presence," as suggested by Aune.

those adhering to the teachings from the Nicolaitans as well. *16* Therefore, repent. But if you don't, I will come to you quickly and make war with them by means of the sword from my mouth. *17* Let he who has an ear hear what the Spirit says to the churches: to the victor, I will give him some of the hidden manna, and I will give him a white stone, and upon the stone a new name will have been written, which no one knows except the one receiving it.

Introduction of the Audience and the Author

Pergamum was home of a grand temple of Zeus, and it was also a focus of Caesar-worship. The temple itself looked like a throne, which is one reason why it is referred to as a seat or throne of Satan. Pergamum was known as the city of the sword because the government of Pergamum had the right to execute without an appeal to Rome. Pergamum had the first medical school known to Western history. At one time, Pergamum had the second-greatest library in the Western world after Alexandria and developed the process of recording writings on animal skins rather than papyri, but Mark Antony gave this library away to Cleopatra. However, in NT times Pergamum was still a center of education, striving to retain its place of importance.[76]

To this church, located in "the city of the sword" and noted for having many members who had gone after false teachers/teachings, Jesus introduces Himself in Revelation 2:12 as ὁ ἔχων τὴν ῥομφαίαν τὴν δίστομον τὴν ὀξεῖαν (*ho echōn tēn rhomphaian tēn distomon tēn oxeian*) "the One having the sharp, two-edged sword." Some of the significance of this title was explored above in consideration of Rev 1:16. Later in this letter to Pergamum (in Rev 2:16), Jesus Christ gives a very specific application for this title: if the Pergamenes fail to repent, He will use the sword from His mouth to make war against those following the false teachers/teachings.

Acknowledgement of the Pergamenes' Faithfulness Under Hardships

Pergamum is referred to as the throne of Satan in Rev 2:13 due to a confluence of several local features. As mentioned above, the altar of Zeus, who was said to be king of the gods, resembled a throne. Also, Caesar-worship was prominent in Pergamum, and failure to pay homage to Caesar

---

[76] Daniel E. Hatfield, "Revelation 2:12-17" (classroom lecture notes, *22440–Greek Syntax and Exegesis*, Spring 2007).

was considered high treason against the state.[77] Rampant paganism and blasphemous nationalism led to severe, satanic persecution of the church, as illustrated in the case of Antipas.

Who is the "Antipas" mentioned in the text? Simeon Metaphrastes, a tenth century Christian who collected stories of martyrs, wrote that Antipas was executed by being sealed inside a hollow statue of a bull– made of brass– which had been heated until it was red hot and that Antipas called out prayers and thanksgiving from inside the bull. According to Metaphrastes, Antipas was martyred during Domitian's reign (r. AD 81-96). If Metaphrastes can be trusted, this mention of "Antipas" helps to confirm the testimony of Irenaeus (AD 120-202) that Revelation was written "toward the end of Domitian's reign."[78]

On the other hand, some historians (such as Philip Schaff) and Bible commentators (such as Jamieson, Fausset, and Brown) doubt Metaphrastes' identification of Antipas.[79] They

---

[77] Beale, *The Book of Revelation*, 246.

[78] Irenaeus, *Adversus Haereses*, 5.30.3. [on-line]; accessed 28 October 2013; available from http://www.ccel.org/ccel/schaff/anf01.ix.i.html; digital book.

[79] Philip Schaff, *History of the Christian Church Volume 4* [on-line]; accessed 28 October 2013; available from http://www.ccel.org/ccel/schaff/hcc4.i.xiv.v.html; digital book. Robert Jamieson, A.R. Fausset, and David Brown, *Commentary Critical and Explanatory on the Whole Bible* [on-line]; accessed 28 October 2013; available from http://

note that Metaphrastes seems to accept fantastical and dubious accounts uncritically. Furthermore, no written record of Antipas exists from the time between Revelation and Metaphrastes; therefore, no one can check the sources of his account. For these reasons, those who argue for an earlier date of Revelation (during Nero's reign, AD 54-68) do not accept Metaphrastes' account as reliable evidence against their position.[80]

"Antipas" is mentioned in Rev 2:13 as someone whose sacrifice was well-known to the entire Pergamene congregation. "Antipas" literally means "against all:" this may have been a nickname by which the martyr was known due to his stand for the Faith against intense opposition. Antipas "was killed in [the] presence" of the Pergamene believers: this term probably indicates that the wicked authorities executed Antipas as an example and warning to other Christians. Yet even seeing Antipas slain, the Pergamene Christians refused to deny the "Faith."[81] "Faith" is used in Rev 2:13 to indicate the gospel, or good news, about Jesus. Having died for his refusal to deny the Faith,

---

www.biblestudytools.com/commentaries/jamieson-fausset-brown/revelation/revelation-2.html; digital book.

[80] For a defense of dating Revelation during Nero's reign, see K.L. Gentry, *Before Jerusalem Fell* (Tyler: Institute for Christian Economics, 1989).

[81] Jesus says, τὴν πίστιν μου (*tēn pistin mou*) = "my Faith," or, "the Faith concerning me."

Antipas has the honor of Jesus calling him ὁ πιστός μου (*ho pistos mou*) "my faithful one." Jesus also calls Antipas "my witness;" "witness" is a translation of the Greek word μαρτύς (*martyr*), and the use of this word in relation to Antipas' death is one of the early indications for the reason why "martyr" came to mean "one who dies for his or her beliefs."

Condemnation of the Pergamenes' Tolerance of the Balaamites

In contrast to the Smyrnean congregation, which had likewise suffered persecution and received no rebuke, Jesus– after encouraging the Pergamenes– tells them ἀλλ᾽ ἔχω κατὰ σοῦ ὀλίγα (*all echo kata sou oliga*) "but I have a few things against you." Jesus rebukes the Pergamenes for their tolerance of those who hold to false teachings: κρατοῦντας τὴν διδαχὴν Βαλαάμ (*kratountas tēn didachēn Balaam*) "those adhering to the teachings of Balaam" and κρατοῦντας τὴν διδαχὴν [τῶν] Νικολαϊτῶν (*kratountas tēn didachēn [tōn] Nikolaitōn*) "those adhering to the teachings of the Nicolaitans."

The reference to the teachings of Balaam in Rev 2:14 seems to be indicating Numbers 31:16, in which Balaam is said to provide counsel that resulted in the Israelites committing sexual immorality and practicing idolatry. In Pergamum, there was apparently a group encouraging participation in the orgiastic idol feasts by teaching that such activity was permissible for Christians. Perhaps part of the motivation for the teachers' attitudes was either the threat of economic depravation or the promise of financial gain, as the promise of treasure to Balaam plays such a prominent role in the biblical account and subsequent traditions.[82]

Condemnation of the Pergamenes' Tolerance of the Nicolaitans

Jesus mentions another sect in Revelation 2:15. In addition to those holding to the teaching of Balaam, the Pergamene church had others holding to the teaching of the Nicolaitans.[83] In contrast to the Ephesian church, the church at Pergamum tolerated the Nicolaitans' teachings/works.[84]

Admonition to the Pergamenes

The command to "repent" in Revelation 2:16 is given in the second person singular. This direct address personalizes the command to everyone

---

[82] Beale, *The Book of Revelation*, 249.

[83] Thomas, *Revelation 1-7*, 194.

[84] For more on the Nicolaitans, see comments on Rev 2:6 above.

in the Pergamene church as they heard the letter read aloud: each person should examine himself/ herself to see if he or she is tolerating the teachings of the Balaamites/Nicolaitans. On the other hand, there is certainly a corporate dimension to this command to "repent" as well: the letter is directly addressed to the "angel [i.e., messenger] of the church in Pergamum," and it is intended for the entire church (Rev 1:11). This seems to indicate that repentance is to take the form of the church pursuing a process of discipline with those who are holding to the teaching of the Nicolaitans or the Balaamites.[85]

Warning to the Pergamenes

If the Pergamenes fail to examine their lives individually, and if they fail to exercise church discipline against those who will not repent, then Jesus warns them in Revelation 2:16 that– "Just as

---

[85] Hamilton, *Revelation*, 90. While I use the term "Balaamites" both in this chapter and in the outline as a kind of shorthand, notice that the text reads, "those adhering to the teachings of Balaam." Unlike those identified as the "Nicolaitans"– a term that seems to be a proper, self-given name for a group– those who Jesus identifies as following the teachings of Balaam did not likely refer to themselves as "Balaamites," nor did any leader of the group likely refer to himself as "Balaam:" a name which carries the negative connotations explored above. By invoking the name of "Balaam," Jesus exposes the true character of the group.

the Lord struck down those who yoked themselves to the Baal of Peor, and 24,000 died (Numbers 25:9);"[86] just as the Israelites killed Balaam by the sword (Numbers 31:8)[87]– He will go to war with those holding to the teachings of the Balaamites or Nicolaitans. The threatened "sword" that may be used in war against the Balaamites or Nicolaitans is said to be "from [Jesus'] mouth," emphasizing that the judgment of these heretical groups is by the Lord's direct command and that their error will be overthrown by the truth He speaks. Similar to the judgment that is threatened in this passage, in Rev 19:21 Jesus is again presented as the One who defeats His enemies by the sword from His mouth.

Charge to Heed the Word

Observe again that "churches" in Rev 2:17 is in the plural, even though it is the church in Pergamum that is currently being addressed. The promise is extended to each "victor"– each one who is faithful to the end– no matter whether or not that "victor" is located in Pergamum. Likewise, the rest of the letter should be considered as applicable to other churches. For example, it is obvious from

---

[86] Ibid.

[87] The word translated "sword" in the LXX of this passage is ῥομφαίᾳ (*rhomphaia*), the same word used for "sword" in Rev 2:16.

the above letter to Ephesus (Rev 2:1-7) that the heresy of the Nicolaitans was a danger in places other than Pergamum.

Promise to the Victor

In Revelation 2:17, the one who is faithful to the end despite persecution and who does not tolerate the teachings of the Balaamites/Nicolaitans is promised τοῦ μάννα τοῦ κεκρυμμένου (*tou manna tou kekrummenou*) "the hidden manna" and ψῆφον λευκήν (*psēphon leukēn*) "a white stone." "The hidden manna" is an allusion to the jar of manna held within the Ark of the Covenant (Exo 16:32-34) and is employed in contrast to the food sacrificed to idols previously mentioned in Rev 2:14.[88]

In connection with the earlier OT references informing the readers' understanding of the rewards to be given, the white stones with names engraved upon them seem to recall the stones worn by the high priest, bearing the names of the children of Israel before the LORD (Exo 39:6-14), which is consistent with the already-established idea of the priesthood of all believers. These stones are characterized both by their whiteness– "whiteness" in Revelation is consistently a metaphor for righteousness[89]– and by the inscription of a "new

---

[88] Thomas, *Revelation 1-7*, 194.

[89] Beale, *The Book of Revelation*, 253.

name" upon them. The "new name" is properly understood, not in terms of each believer receiving an individual secret name for himself/herself, but– in connection with Rev 19:12– the "new name" is a name for Christ, which no one will know until the final judgment, and then only those who are victorious through faith in Christ will know this name. Unbelievers will never know this hidden name of the Lord;[90] knowledge of this name speaks of a special, loving relationship between the Lord and His faithful followers.

---

[90] Ibid., 257.

Chapter Seven

Letter to the Church in Thyatira (Rev 2:18-29)

18 And write to the angel of the church in Thyatira:

Thus says the Son of God, having eyes like a flame of fire and feet resembling fine bronze:

19 I know your works– your goodness, faithfulness, service, and perseverance[91]– and that your last works surpass your first [works].[92] **20** But I have this against you: you tolerate the woman Jezebel, who calls herself a prophetess and teaches, and she seduces my servants to fornicate and to eat meat sacrificed to an idol. **21** And I gave her some time[93] so that she

---

[91] The list of accusatives (τὴν ἀγάπην-τὴν ὑπομονήν) are taken as describing the "works."

[92] The referent of "first" at the end of the sentence is the same as that of "last" earlier in the sentence, and so "works" is added in the translation for clarity.

[93] χρόνον, which is literally rendered "a time," in translated to mean "some time."

might repent, but[94] she doesn't want to repent from her fornication. **22** Look! I will throw her into a sick-bed and those committing adultery with her into great affliction, unless they repent from her evil works. **23** And I will destroy her children in a plague. And all the churches will know that I am the searcher of minds and hearts, and I will give to each of you according to your works. **24** But to the rest of you in Thyatira– as many as don't keep her teaching: whosoever doesn't know "the deep things of Satan" (as they say)– I tell you: I will not place another burden upon you, **25** except [that you[95]] hold fast to what you have until I come. **26** And to the victor, the one keeping my works, I will give him authority over the nations. **27** And he will rule them with an iron rod; he will shatter them like ceramic pots– **28** as I also receive [authority] from my Father– and I will give him the morning star. **29** Let he who has an ear hear what the Spirit says to the churches.

---

[94] The second καὶ in this verse is taken as adversative, and it is thus translated "but" (Aune, *Revelation*, 197).

[95] The subject of the phrase has been re-iterated in the translation for clarity.

Introduction of the Audience and the Author

Thyatira was an industrial town on inland Asia Minor. The town was by a river on a plain and had no natural defenses. The town was often subject to fires due to its many foundries. This was the least important city (imperially speaking), and yet the longest letter, in Revelation 2-3. The church in Thyatira was subject to persecution due to the trade guilds, which controlled all the business in the town and which were run like powerful fraternities, with degrading initiation rites, debauchery, and frequent hazing.[96]

To Thyatira, Jesus refers to himself in Rev 2:18 as "the Son of God" then uses imagery drawn from Rev 1:14-15. To this church in which many were engaged in "fornication," Jesus emphasizes His divinity, and that He has "eyes like a flame of fire"– indicating that He can see their deeds of darkness (cf. Eph 5:11) through His omniscience– and "feet resembling fine bronze"– indicating His holy purity. Jesus, the Son of God, perfectly knows of the Thyatirans' sinful acts and He remains set apart from those committing those acts.

---

[96] Daniel E. Hatfield, "Revelation 2:18-29" (classroom lecture notes, *22440–Greek Syntax and Exegesis*, Spring 2007).

Commendation of the Thyatirans' works

The works for which the Thyatirans are commended in Rev 2:19 are indeed impressive. These works are defined in terms of "goodness, faithfulness, service, and perseverance." Like the Ephesians, the Thyatirans had "not tired out" (Rev 2:3); in fact, the Thyatirans' "last works surpass [their] first [works]." Their works had not ceased prior to the writing of this letter; they had persevered and increased in serving others. Their works were characterized by "goodness," which in this case must indicate a kind of selflessness. Nor were their works devoid of gospel witness; otherwise, Jesus would not have commended them for their "faithfulness."

In spite of all this, however, the Thyatirans receive a stern rebuke from the Son of God. Due to the influence of "Jezebel," many of the Thyatiran Christians had begun to engage in idolatry and sexual immorality. These gross sins threatened to undermine all of the good that the Thyatirans had done in the name of Christ. The Thyatirans' good works (as good as they truly were) could not save them, and Jesus (with "eyes like a flame of fire") would not wink at their sin.

Condemnation of the Thyatirans' Tolerance of Jezebel

τὴν γυναῖκα Ἰεζάβελ (*tēn gunaika Iezabel*) "the woman Jezebel" almost certainly refers to a certain individual within the congregation at Thyatira rather than to a sect in general, as the singular "woman" is used in Revelation 2:20, and it would be awkward symbolism for the entire sect to be spoken of as claiming to be "a [singular] prophetess." In previous sections, groups were referred to as "those adhering to the teachings of Balaam" (Rev 2:14) or "those adhering to the teachings of the Nicolaitans" (Rev 2:15), not by an individual person's name. Also, groups of mixed gender in the Bible are normally referred to using masculine terms, and the punishment for "Jezebel" is differentiated somewhat from the punishment of "her children" (taken to mean "her followers") in subsequent verses.

Prophetesses are mentioned a few places in the NT record. The word for prophetess is used of Anna in Luke 2:36 and the daughters of Philip are said to prophesy in Acts 21:9. In the apostolic era, prophets ranked only behind apostles in their importance to the church. The "Jezebel" in Thyatira was obviously accepted into the congregation of Thyatira as a prophetess, but she used her position to lead others astray. She is referred to as Jezebel (though this was unlikely a name she used of herself, as it had consistently negative associations for God's people), bringing to mind the OT queen of Israel, who is identified with harlotry and witchcraft (2 Kings 9:22); the OT Jezebel promoted the worship of foreign gods.

Impending Judgment Against Jezebel and Her Followers

Idolatry and fornication were closely related in biblical times. "Religious infidelity is often spoken of in the OT under the figure of harlotry (e.g., Jer 3:6; Eze 23:19; Hos 9:1)."[97] Idolatry such as that to which Jezebel enticed Israel in the OT was often accompanied by literal sexual perversion, and idolatry was not much different in this respect during NT times. The fornication that is mentioned in Rev 2:20 in association with other cultic practices, and which is mentioned later in this book alongside idolatry three times (Rev 19:21; 21:8; 22:15), cannot be understood as something entirely spiritual, but literal sexual immorality is also in view.

"Jezebel" herself was given time to repent, but she refused (Rev 2:21). Her followers are warned strongly that they must repent. μετανοήσωσιν (*metanoēsōsin*) "repent," preceded by ἐὰν μὴ (*ean*

---

97 Thomas, *Revelation 1-7*, 218.

mē) "unless" in Rev 2:22, is a negative third class conditional clause indicating that, as things stand, it is probable that those committing adultery– like "Jezebel" herself– will not repent, and so they will receive judgment.

The judgment of which Jezebel's "children" are warned in Revelation 2:23 is rather specific. Jesus had warned the Ephesians that failure to repent would result in His coming to "remove [their] lamp-stand from its place" (Rev 2:5), but the process of this lamp-stand removal [understood in terms of the Ephesian congregation losing its status as a true church of Christ: see the above commentary] was left rather vague. Likewise, those in the church of Pergamum were warned that if they did not repent concerning those following the "teachings of Balaam" and the "teachings of the Nicolaitans," Jesus would come to "make war with them by means of the sword from [His] mouth" (Rev 2:16), and this "war" is certainly a picture of violent destruction, but the exact way in which this destruction would come about was left a bit unclear. In Rev 2:23, Jesus says, ἀποκτενῶ ἐν θανάτῳ (*apoktenō en thanatō*): although this phrase could be a Hebraism meaning "I will certainly kill," the difference in the words (rather than the normal manner of using cognates to express intensification), the strong similarity of this phrase to Eze 33:27 in the LXX (wherein דֶבֶר, the word for "plague," or "pestilence, is translated with a form of θανατος), and the later Greek use of θανατικό to mean "disease" all seem to indicate that this phrase should be translated, "I will destroy... in a plague." As may be expected, those who engage in regular fornication are fated to fall in deadly disease.

One reason that Jesus is a bit more specific in His warning concerning Jezebel and her followers is because He intends this impending judgment to serve as a warning to the members of other churches that He, the Son of God with "eyes like a flame of fire," is "the searcher of minds and hearts," and the fulfillment of a specific prophesy would serve as a more stark warning to others. The phrase "minds and hearts" is νεφοὺς καὶ καρδίας (*nephous kai kardias*), literally "kidneys and hearts:" this refers to the entire spiritual/ mental/ emotional/volitional component of a person. This forms part of an allusion to Jeremiah 17:10: the statement from Jeremiah is especially applicable to the congregation in Thyatira because Jeremiah, like John, was dealing with people who were practicing idolatry due to economic motives (cf. Jer 17:3, 11; 11:10-17, 20).[98]

---

[98] Beale, *The Book of Revelation*, 264.

Encouragement to the Remnant in Thyatira

τὰ βαθέα τοῦ Σατανᾶ (*ta bathea tou Satana*) "the deep things of Satan" in Rev 2:24, followed by the quotation formula, ὡς λέγουσιν (*hōs legousin*) "as they say," was apparently a phrase actually employed by "Jezebel" and her followers, as incredible as this may seem. Some have tried to understand ὡς λέγουσιν (*hōs legousin*) "as they say" as applying to the faithful group in Thyatira, so that τὰ βαθέα τοῦ Σατανᾶ (*ta bathea tou Satana*) "the deep things of Satan" is an accusation made by the godly against "Jezebel"'s followers. On the other hand, the Lord, in this section, is addressing the godly in the second person, and λέγουσὶν is in the third person, so the phrase must be used by a group other than the faithful Thyatirans.

Others have tried to understand τοῦ Σατανα (*tou Satana*) "of Satan" as an addition to– or substitute for– part of a phrase that was actually employed by the Jezebelite sect. This would be grammatically absurd, however, as ὡς λέγουσιν (*hōs legousin*) "as they say" introduces a phrase that– in its entirety– would be understood as a quote from the third party.

τὰ βαθέα τοῦ Σατανᾶ (*ta bathea tou Satana*) "the deep things of Satan" were actually taught, under this name, by later Gnostic sects such as the Cainites, Carpocratians, and Naasenes. The Jezebelites seem to have adopted an early form of this error. They believed themselves impervious to any spiritual danger from sin, so they claimed to participate in τὰ βαθέα τοῦ Σατανᾶ (*ta bathea tou Satana*) "the deep things of Satan"– such as the fornications and participation in idolatrous festivals previously mentioned– in order to prove their freedom from any hint of legalism.

Admonition to the Remnant in Thyatira

To those in Thyatira who have not followed Jezebel in her perverse practices and principles, Jesus says, οὐ βάλλω ἐφ᾽ ὑμᾶς ἄλλο βάρος, πλὴν ὃ ἔχετε κρατήσατε ἄχρι[ς] οὗ ἄν ἥξω (*ou ballō eph humas allo baros plēn ho exhete kratēsate achri[s] hou an hēxō*) "I will not place another burden upon you, except hold fast to what you have until I come." As seen in Rev 2:19, the Thyatiran church excelled in genuine good works. With a plague about to hit many people in their congregation, the faithful Thyratirans may have been tempted to think that the effects of this plague could be lessened if they did even more good deeds. This is a burden Jesus does not want them to bear.

Similar to his condemnation of the Pergamenes' tolerance for the Nicolaitans and Balaamites (Rev 2:14-15), Jesus had condemned the Thyatirans' tolerance of Jezebel and her followers, yet in contrast to His admonition to the church in Pergamum, Jesus does not command the Thyatirans as a whole to "repent" (Rev 2:16). The reason, apparently, is that the situation in Thyatira has become so bad, and the judgment against Jezebel and her followers is so near, that the church in Thyatira will not have the opportunity to begin exercising church discipline.[99]

Promise to the Victor

Jesus promises to give the faithful victor, ἐουσίαν ἐπὶ τῶν ἐθνῶν (*exousian epi tōn ethnōn*) "authority over the nations." This phrase begins an allusion in Revelation 2:26b-27 to Psalm 2:8-9 (especially in the words of the LXX).[100] Psalm 2 is Messianic in nature, promising that the Messiah will receive authority over the nations. The Thyatirans who keep Christ's works– persevering through temptation and persecution as He did– will also participate in Christ's rule.

The Lord Jesus Christ, who declares Himself to be the morning star in Revelation 22:16, here promises to give the morning star to those who

---

[99]   The 'coming' in Rev 2:25 should primarily be understood in the context of Jesus coming in judgment against Jezebel and her followers.

[100] Aune, *Revelation 1-5*, 209.

overcome and keep His works. The "morning star" (Venus) was a symbol of sovereignty in the ancient world; this was especially true in Rome, where the emperor claimed to be a descendant of the goddess Venus.[101] Jesus claims to be the true ruler– and to make His persecuted followers into true rulers– in spite of the claims of the present world system. The promise that the victor will receive "the morning star" continues the idea of believers participating in the reign of Christ. The ideas in Revelation 2:26-28– of the Messiah (and, by His extension of grace, those in Christ) ruling with an iron rod or scepter and manifested in brilliance like the morning star– are ancient, as seen in the prophecy spoken through Balaam in Numbers 24:17. Significantly, 2 Peter 1:17-19 refers to "the morning star" arising in believers' hearts immediately after a reference to Psalm 2.

Charge to Heed the Word

Jesus places the charge, "Let he who has an ear hear what the Spirit says to the churches," after the promise to the victor in the structure of the last four letters (beginning here in Revelation 2:29), though this charge comes before the promise to the victor in the structure of the first three letters. Having established that all the churches should

---

[101] Beale, *The Book of Revelation*, 269.

heed the message that is given to each church–
that the message to each particular congregation
is applicable to every believer– the repeated charge
to heed the word is now more of an afterthought.
However, Jesus continues to include this charge
at the end of every letter so that no believer can
mistakenly conclude that the message to any
church is not relevant in his or her life.

Chapter Eight

Letter to the Church in Sardis (Rev 3:1-6)

1 And write to the angel of the church in Sardis:

Thus says the One having the sevenfold Spirit of God and the seven stars:

I know your works: that you have a name that you are alive, but you are dead. *2* Become vigilant and strengthen those remaining things, which were about to die, for I have found that your works have not been fulfilled in the presence of my God. *3* Therefore, remember how you have received and heard; keep [it] and repent. If you are not vigilant, I will come as a thief, and you do not expect what hour I will come against you. *4* But you have a few names in Sardis who have not dirtied their clothes, and they will walk with me in white, because they are worthy. *5* Thus the victor will be dressed in white clothes and I will certainly not erase his name from the book of life, and I will declare his name in the presence of my Father and in the presence of his angels. **6** Let he who has an ear hear what the Spirit says to the churches.

Introduction of the Audience and the Author

Sardis was "the citadel of the plain" on the Pactolus River. The town was a natural fortress due to geography, and it was surrounded by rich farmland, so it could withstand a prolonged siege. The city previously had been destroyed by the Persians, however, and then by the Greeks 300 years later.[102] These times of destruction had come due to the city failing to keep adequate watch.[103]

Jesus introduces Himself in Revelation 3:1 to the church in Sardis as ὁ ἔχων τὰ ἑπτὰ πνεύματα τοῦ θεοῦ καὶ τοὺς ἑπτὰ ἀστέρας (*ho echōn ta hepta pneumata tou theou kai tous hepta asteras*) "the One having the sevenfold Spirit of God and the seven stars." This title once again emphasizes Jesus' sovereignty over the churches. In particular, this title draws special attention to the fact that the message sent to the church is from Jesus Himself. It is Jesus Himself who holds the seven stars, which He identifies with the angels

---

[102] Daniel E. Hatfield, "Revelation 3:1-6" (classroom lecture notes, *22440–Greek Syntax and Exegesis*, Spring 2007).

[103] Gregg, *Revelation: Four Views*, 73.

to the various churches (Rev 1:20), and which I have argued should be understood in context as those reading the letters to the churches. Jesus Himself holds the sevenfold Spirit of God: the Spirit who– at the end of each letter– is said to be speaking to the churches through the letter. When the church in Sardis hears this letter they are not to understand it as the mere words of men, but as the voice of the Lord Himself.

Condemnation of the Sardians' Deadness

In the letters to Ephesus (Rev 2:2-3), Pergamum (Rev 2:13), and Thyatira (Rev 2:19), Jesus commends some aspect of the church's ministry– or, in the case of Pergamum, acknowledges the church's faithfulness under hardships– before condemning some aspect of the church's practice. The form of Jesus' address to the church in Sardis stands in stark contrast to this pattern. After introducing Himself in Rev 3:1a, Jesus immediately issues a condemnation. And this condemnation is harsh indeed. The church in Thyatira and even the church in Ephesus had significant problems, but at least they had consistent, godly works for which they could be commended. The works of the church in Sardis, on the other hand, appear as sheer hypocrisy. Like the scribes and Pharisees, who Jesus had described as "whitewashed sepulchers"– having a beautiful outward appearance, but full of dead men's bones (Matt 23:27)– the church in Sardis had a name that they were alive, but (in general, see Rev 3:4) they were dead.

ὄνομα (*onoma*) "name" is mentioned four times in the letter to Sardis. In Rev 3:1, the Sardians' are said to have a "name" that they are alive, but Jesus exposes this "name" as false. On the other hand, in Rev 3:4 Jesus declares that the church in Sardis has "a few names... who have not dirtied their clothes." These faithful Sardiceans– and all others who are victorious– will not have their names blotted out from the book of life (Rev 3:5a). Jesus will declare the names of His faithful ones before His Father and the angels (Rev 3:5b). Through this contrast in how "name" is used, Jesus differentiates between the hypocrites who have a name before men and those who are truly faithful, who have their names recognized in the book of life and declared before God and His heavenly host.

Unlike the situations in Pergamum and Thyatira, the church in Sardis does not seem to have a problem with allowing heretical teachings/ teachers in their midst. Their problem does not appear to be doctrinal, but practical. Jesus condemned the heart condition of the Ephesian church because they had "left [their] first love" (Rev 2:4) and ceased doing "the first works" (Rev 2:5) of gospel proclamation. The church in Sardis has similar problems, but to an even more extreme degree. They were regularly going through the motions of devotion to Christ, and they had avoided heresy (hence their sterling reputation), but they had abandoned heart-devotion to their Lord and most of them had "dirtied their clothes."[104]

Admonition to the Sardians

In Revelation 3:2, Jesus admonishes the church in Sardis with five commands: γίνου γρηγορῶν (*ginou grēgorōn*) "become vigilant," στήρισον (*stērison*) "strengthen," μνημόνευε (*mnēmoneue*) "remember," τήρει (*tērei*) "keep," and μετανόησον (*metanoēson*) "repent."

The church in Sardis must first "become vigilant."[105] The church in Sardis had been lulled into a type of slumber: considering themselves to be just fine, when in fact they were in a grave state. Their self-misperception was reinforced by the fact that they had somehow obtained a reputation of being alive, despite their true deadness. In order to benefit from any of Jesus' other admonitions, warnings, encouragements, or promises, the

---

[104] See the explanation of Rev 3:4 below.

[105] Note that this command would have called to mind the city's history of having been previously destroyed due to a lack of vigilance.

church in Sardis must first wake up and be alert as to their actual condition.

Upon becoming vigilant, the church in Sardis must "strengthen:" in particular, they must "strengthen those remaining things, which were about to die." With this command, Jesus' pronouncement from Rev 3:1 that the church in Sardis is "dead"– a pronouncement that seems so final and hopeless, and that is surely calculated to alarm the Sardian church so that they become "vigilant" (Rev 3:2)– is somewhat tempered: the church does have some "remaining things," which are not yet quite dead. Yet the situation remains dire: these "remaining things" are "about to die," lacking an inner vitality. The Sardian congregation must certainly have begun many good works in order to gain the false reputation of being a vibrant church, but these works are incomplete.

In order to strengthen the remaining commendable features of their congregation and to complete or fulfill their works in the presence of God, the church in Sardis must "remember," "keep," and "repent." The command to "remember" echoes the command given to the Ephesian church in Rev 2:5. The Ephesian Christians are commanded to "remember from where you have fallen" (understood in terms of their commitment to gospel proclamation[106]) and the Sardian

---

[106] See the explanation in Chapter 4 above.

Christians are commanded to "remember how you have received and heard" (a phrase that must be understood in terms of their reception of the gospel message). The works of the Sardian Christians are incomplete and "about to die" because the church in Sardis has generally forgotten the gospel. The good news of who Jesus is and what He has done on behalf of sinners has become peripheral in the lives of the Sardian Christians, rather than the core motivation of their works.

Upon remembering how they received and heard, the church in Sardis must "keep [it]." The command to "keep" "how you received and heard" is exceedingly strange in translation. This command must be understood in terms of the Sardian congregation consistently dwelling upon the memory of how the gospel was proclaimed to them: allowing gospel proclamation to inform every action performed by the church.

The true solution for the Sardians' deadness lies in repentance: turning from dead works to a living relationship with Jesus based on the gospel they had heard. Out of the seven churches Jesus addresses in Rev 2-3, four are commanded to repent: Ephesus (Rev 2:5), Pergamum (Rev 2:16), Sardis (Rev 3:3), and Laodicea (Rev 3:19). The churches in Smyrna and Philadelphia are not commanded to repent because they are remaining faithful through persecution. The church in

Thyatira is not commanded to repent because the heretical element in the church has already been given time for repentance and now their judgment is eminent. The command to repent is a blessing: another gracious opportunity for the church to strengthen and complete their works in God's presence before they face His judgment.

Warning to the Sardians

If the Sardian Christians fail to wake up to their true condition (repentance is implied here in Rev 3:3 as well), then Jesus will come against them as a thief. In the letters to the Pergamene and Thyatiran Christians, the warnings about Christ's coming judgment were specifically focused on heretical groups. The Sardian church's problem— characterized as a state of deadness– is widespread throughout the church. Jesus' coming against the Sardians should be understood in similar terms as His coming to the Ephesians in judgment to remove their lamp-stand (Rev 2:5). If the church in Sardis does not wake up and repent, finding life rather than death, then they will suddenly cease to exist as a church.

Encouragement to the Remnant in Sardis

Those remaining faithful in Sardis are characterized in Rev 3:4 as ὀλίγα (*oliga*) "few." In Pergamum and Thyatira, the faithful were a majority who had, sadly, allowed a heretical minority to have unchecked influence in the congregation. In Sardis the "dead"– those who are not practicing vigilance, who are allowing their works to become feeble, who are not remembering or keeping the gospel central, and who are yet unrepentant– are the majority of the congregation.

"Clothes" or "garments" often symbolize works or witness in Revelation.[107] The "dead" majority of the Sardians have apparently compromised their works and witness. The church in Sardis is not engaged in any particular act of gross immorality (as seen in the Thyatirans' tolerance of Jezebel), but they are characterized by a general spiritual dinginess, as they have been living for this world rather than for the gospel.

Promise to the Victor

In Revelation 3:5, Jesus promises that the "victor" περιβαλεῖται ἐν ἱματίοις λευκοῖς (*peribaleitai en himatiois leukois*) "will be dressed in white clothes." Believers in Christ have been

---

[107] Hatfield, "Revelation 3:1-6."

made priests (Rev 1:6), and the one who overcomes will be given priestly garments (Lev 16:4).

As seen throughout Revelation, believers in Christ share in the holy things belonging to God. God is depicted as the Ancient of Days in Daniel 7:9 with language that is unmistakably similar to the language used to depict the vision of Christ at the beginning of the Book of Revelation. In Daniel 7:9 the Ancient of Days is wearing a white robe; Jesus, in his transfiguration, is similarly clothed in white (see Mark 9:3). In the end time prophecy at the close of the Book of Daniel, the prophet Daniel is told, "Many shall be purified, made white, and refined" (Dan 12:10). Similarly, Rev 3:5 promises that those who overcome will be clothed in white.

οὐμὴ ἐξαλείψ τὸ ῎ονομα αὐτοῦ ἐκ τῆς βίβλου τῆς ζωῆς (*oumē eksaleips to onoma autou ek tēs biblou tēs zōēs*) "I will certainly not erase his name from the book of life." The idea of a book from which the Lord threatens to erase or blot out the names of the unfaithful is first revealed in Exodus 32:32-33. David wrote a Psalm calling for his enemies to be blotted out of the book of life (see Psa 69:28), and Isaiah wrote of those "recorded for life" in Jerusalem (see Isa 4:3). In the Old Covenant community, each member was recorded on a census, and especially the Levites (Num 1:2; 3:15; Eze 13:9). To have one's name blotted out from the census was to remove one from the blessings of the covenant community. In Rev 3:5 the victor, having his name preserved in the book of life, is promised full realization of the blessings of the New Covenant community.

The "book of life" is mentioned again in Rev 13:8 and 17:8. In these passages, certain names are said to have been written in the book ἀπὸ καταβολῆς κόσμου (*apo kataboles kosmou*) "from the foundation of the world." In Rev 13:8 and 17:8, everyone dwelling upon the earth worships the beast and marvels at the beast. That is: absolutely everyone is deceived by the beast *except* those who have had their names written in the book of life from the foundation of the world. Having one's name written in the book of life from the foundation of the world is thus seen to have a direct preserving effect on souls of the saints. This reality should temper any speculation that words such as those in Rev 3:5 about erasing/blotting out (or *not* erasing/blotting out) names from the book of life may indicate that those who are truly saved may lose their salvation.

The "book of life" plays a prominent role in the great white throne judgment about which John prophesies in Rev 20:11-15. At this judgment, books that record the works of each person are opened. Everyone will be judged according to his or her works. But "another book"– the "book of life"– is also opened (Rev 20:12). This book is most crucial, for it is only through having one's name written in this book that a person will be saved from being "thrown into the lake of fire" (Rev 20:15). Furthermore, it is only through having one's name written in the "book of life" that a person will be allowed to enter into the new Jerusalem (Rev 21:27).

ὁμολογήσω τὸ ὄνομα αὐτοῦ ἐνώπιον τοῦ πετρός μου καὶ ἐνώπιον τῶν ἀγγέλων αὐτοῦ (*homologēsō to onoma autou enōpion tou patros mou kai enōpion tōn angelōn autou*) "I will declare his name in the presence of my Father and in the presence of his angels." This is in accordance with what Jesus promised his followers in Matthew 10:32 and Luke 12:8. As the high priest in OT times bore the names of the tribes on his ephod, our great High Priest bears our individual names before God.

If our names will be declared before God the Father, who is supremely important, why even mention "the presence of his angels"? Those from the church in Sardis who had "dirtied their clothes" through compromise with the world– and those like them even in churches today– are concerned with receiving public praise. What they forfeit through their sin is not only a secret commendation before God the Father but also the most spectacular display of public praise imaginable, as the faithful will be honored "in the presence of His angels."

Charge to Heed the Word

The regular charge is again placed at the end of this letter in Rev 3:6: "Let he who has an ear hear what the Spirit says to the churches." The original Sardian hearers of this letter would have taken special interest in this charge for two reasons. First, given the command they had received to be vigilant and the warning they had been given for failure to attain vigilance, this command to "hear" would have seemed especially pointed. Second, given the introduction of Jesus as "the One having the sevenfold Spirit of God" (Rev 3:1), this explicit reference to the Spirit speaking in the letter would have reinforced the fact that the commands they have received in this letter were from God Himself.

Chapter Nine

Letter to the Church in Philadelphia (Rev 3:7-13)

7 And write to the angel of the church in Philadelphia:

The holy one, the true one, the one holding the key of David– the one opening and no one will shut, and shutting and no one will open– says these things:

8 I know your works– *Behold! I have placed before you a door having been opened, which no one can shut*– that[108] you have a little power yet you have kept my word and have not denied my name. 9 Behold! I will deliver some out from the synagogue of Satan (those calling themselves Jews, when they're nothing but liars). Behold! I will force them so that they will come and they will grovel at your feet. And they will know that I loved you. 10 Because you kept my word about perseverance, I will also keep you from the hour of affliction that is about to come

---

[108] ὅτι is "that" rather than "because" as it describes the known works following the parenthetical statement.

upon the entirety of humankind: to test those dwelling upon the earth. *11* I will come quickly; hold fast to what you have, so that no one might take your crown. *12* I will make the victor a pillar in the temple of my God and he shall certainly not depart from it. And furthermore, I will write upon him the name of my God, the name of the city of my God (the new Jerusalem descending out of heaven from my God), and my new name. *13* Let he who has an ear hear what the Spirit says to the churches.

Introduction of the Audience and the Author

Philadelphia was a military outpost of Greece, settled by retired military personnel, who were given land and planted vineyards. Due to military need and Italian pressure, Philadelphia was forced to stop wine production and begin growing corn. Philadelphia was destroyed by an earthquake in A.D. 62 and subsequently existed as a tent city. Philadelphia was known as the "city of the door" as it was a gateway city in ancient times and as it was historically at the farthest reaches of Greek society.[109]

In the last two of the seven letters from Revelation 2-3, Jesus breaks the form established in the first five letters, and He introduces Himself with titles *not* drawn from John's perception of His glorified form, as recorded in Rev 1:9-20. The additional titles by which Jesus introduces Himself to the churches of Philadelphia and Laodicea are rich in theological significance. These titles demonstrate that there is more to Christ than can be comprehended by the human mind in any single vision or series of visions.

To the church in Philadelphia, Jesus introduces Himself in Rev 3:7 as, "The holy one, the true one, the one holding the key of David." ο ἅγιος (*ho hagios*) "the holy one" is used throughout the NT as a title for the Messiah (Mark 1:24; Luke 1:35; 4:34; John 6:69; Acts 4:27,30; 1 John 2:20).[110] ο ἀληθινός (*ho alēthinos*) "the true one" in this context "carries connotations of Jesus being the true Messiah, who has begun to fulfill messianic prophecy, though He is rejected by the Jews as a false messianic pretender."[111] ο ἔχων τὴν κλεῖν Δαυίδ (*ho echōn tēn klein Dauid*) "the one holding the key of David"

---

[109] Daniel E. Hatfield, "Revelation 3:7-13" (classroom lecture notes, *22440—Greek Syntax and Exegesis*, Spring 2007).

[110] Thomas, *Revelation 1-7*, 273.

[111] Beale, *The Book of Revelation*, 283.

is a direct allusion to Isaiah 22:22, and the phrase indicates that Jesus has the true authority of the Davidic covenant. As God had disposed with unrighteous leadership and established Eliakim (see Isa 22), God rejects the wicked rulers of the "synagogue of Satan" (see Rev 3:9) and establishes Christ as sovereign over His Church.[112]

Commendation of the Philadelphians' Works

ἰδοὺ δέδωκα ἐνώπιόν σου θύπαν ἠνεῳγμένην, ἣν οὐδεὶς δύναται κλεῖσαι αὐτήν (*idou dedōka enopion sou thupan ēneōigmenēn, hēn oudeis dunatai kleisai autēn*) "Behold! I have placed before you a door having been opened, which no one can shut" in Revelation 3:8 is a parenthetical phrase set between the usual formula of Christ stating that the congregation's works are known by Him— ᾿οιδά σου τὰ ᾿εργα (*oida sou ta erga*) "I know your works"— and the content of the known works, introduced by ᾿οτι (*hoti*) "that," as in Rev 3:1 and Rev 3:15. This phrase is a specific application of the explanatory phrase of the previous verse: Jesus does not only have the key of David— with the ability to open and shut— in a theoretical sense, but

---

[112] Jesus uses His authority to "open" and "shut"— allowing or disallowing access to God— as explored in the commentary on Rev 3:8 concerning the 'open door'.

He uses His power and authority for the present good of His people. With this phrase, the Lord prefaces the content of the Philadelphians' works (which, to this point, have been marked by "little power") by giving a specific, present hope serving to spur them to greater works.

The 'open door' metaphor may indicate an opportunity for effective gospel witness, as this is how Paul and Luke consistently speak of 'open doors' in rest of the NT (see Acts 14:27; 1 Cor 16:9; 2 Cor 2:12; Col 4:3).[113] On the other hand, John seems to consistently use the metaphor of a "door" or an 'open door' to indicate access to God's presence (see Rev 4:1; John 10:9).[114] Jesus allows the faithful Philadelphians into God's presence while barring the persecutors– who erroneously imagine themselves to be righteous– from His presence.

Encouragement to the Philadelphians

The phrase ἐκ τῆς συναγωγῆς τοῦ Σατανᾶ τῶν λεγόντων ἑαυτοὺς Ἰουδαίους ἒιναι, καὶ οὐκ εἰσὶν ἀλλὰ ψεύδονται (*ek tēs sunagōgēs tou Satana tōn legontōn heautous Ioudaious einai, kai ouk*

---

[113] Ibid., 286.

[114] Thomas Schreiner, "Promises, Promises," Revelation 3:7-13 (sermon, *Clifton Baptist Church*, 9 November 2008); accessed 1 January 2014; available from http://cliftonbaptist.org/sermons-and-audio/; Internet.

eisin all pseudontai) "out from the synagogue of Satan: those calling themselves Jews, when they're nothing but liars," along with Jesus' introduction to the Philadelphian congregation under clear messianic titles,[115] seems to indicate that the congregation was under persecution from the larger Jewish community, which had rejected Christ. In Revelation 3:9, Jesus encourages the church in Philadelphia with knowledge that though they are now persecuted, they will one day be vindicated in the sight of their persecutors.

Forms of the phrase τοὺς κατοικοῦντας ἐπὶ τῆς γῆς (*tous katoikountas epi tēs gēs*) "those dwelling upon the earth" occur throughout the book of Revelation (6:10; 8:13; 11:10; 12:12; 13:8, 12,14; 14:6; 17:2, 8), always referring to unbelieving persecutors.[116] In Rev 3:10, Jesus promises the Philadelphian congregation, κἀγώ σε τηρήσω ἐκ τῆς ὥρας τοῦ πειρασμοῦ (*kagō se tērēsō ek tēs hōras tou peirasmou*) "I will also keep you from the hour of affliction." Jesus encourages the church in Philadelphia with knowledge that they are not alone in suffering "affliction"– in fact "the entirety of humankind" will suffer affliction (this affliction will provide a final "test [to all] those dwelling

---

[115] Note again the break from the letters to the previous congregations, which were prefaced in language reflecting that revealed in the first chapter of Revelation.

[116] Beale, *The Book of Revelation*, 286.

upon the earth" at a future hour)– but the faithful Philadelphians will be kept from the ultimate period of testing, which must be understood as an aspect of the final judgment.

Admonition to the Philadelphians

Though kept from the full extent of the ultimate "hour of affliction," the Philadelpian church– like the other churches in Asia Minor– must be prepared to stand strong through significant persecution. Therefore, Jesus tells them, ἔρχομαι ταχύ· κράτει ὃ ἔχεις, ἵνα μηδεὶς λάβῃ τὸν στέφανόν σου (*erchomai tachu; kratei ho echeis hina mēdeis labē ton stephanon sou*) "I will come quickly; hold fast to what you have, so that no one might take your crown." In contrast to Revelation 2:5, in which Jesus warns the Ephesian church that (unless they repent) He will come to remove their status as a church, in Rev 3:11 Jesus speaks of his speedy appearance as a comfort to the faithful Philadelphian church. Jesus will "come quickly" to relieve the Philadelphian church members who are under trial, to reward their fidelity, and (it is implied) to punish those who fall away.[117] "'Hold fast' suggests that they will be going through trials

---

[117] Matthew Henry, *The Matthew Henry Study Bible*, ed. A. Kenneth Abraham (Iowa Falls: World Bible Publishers, 1997), 2275.

that will require especially diligent safeguarding of faith."[118] Each word of this letter to the church in Philadelphia is designed to strengthen the Philadelphians' faith in Christ.

Promise to the Victor

The imagery of the victorious Philadelphians being made into temple pillars seems to work on at least two levels. The metaphor indicates that the victor will have a permanent place in the presence of God.[119] Also, στῦλον (*stulon*) "pillar" "was used as a metaphor in Greek (as in English) for persons in important leadership positions."[120] The idea that God would give believers in Christ such a prominent position within the temple is a direct affront against the unbelieving Jews who were persecuting them.

In this passage, Jesus promises the believer γράψω ἐπ᾽ αὐτὸν τὸ ᾽ονομα τοῦ θεοῦ μου (*grapsō ep auton to onoma tou theou mou*) "I will write upon him the name of my God." This promise also works on at least two levels. Even today, if a person

---

[118] Beale, *The Book of Revelation*, 293.

[119] The temple does not refer to a literal temple [in the sense of a single building] because Rev 21:22 tells us "there is no temple" in the new Jerusalem. Thomas Schreiner, "Promises, Promises," Revelation 3:7-13.

[120] R.C. Sproul, *The Reformation Study Bible* (Orlando: Ligonier Ministries, 2005), 1694.

writes his or her name on something, he or she is claiming ownership of that object. Thus, God is claiming ownership of those who have persevered– despite persecution– in proclaiming their loyalty to Him. In Numbers 6:27 the children of Israel are said to have the LORD's name placed upon them.[121] Again, the idea that God would give believers in Christ such a covenant privilege is a direct affront against the unbelieving Jews who were persecuting them.

τῆς καινῆς Ἰερουσαλὴμ (*tēs kainēs Ierousalēm*) "the new Jerusalem" is mentioned three times in Revelation (3:12; 21:2, 10). [122] Christ's words about the new Jerusalem here hearken back to OT prophecies of a renewed Jerusalem, as in (for example) Isaiah 62:2. This is another affront to the unbelieving Jews who were persecuting the church in Philadelphia.

Though emphasizing different aspects of the significance of the name written upon believers, τὸ ὄνομα τοῦ θεοῦ μου καὶ τὸ ὄνομα τῆς πόλεως τοῦ θεοῦ μου... καὶ τὸ ὄνομα μου τὸ καινόν (*to onoma tou theou mou kai to onoma tēs poleōs tou theou mou... kai to onoma mou to kainon*) "the name of my God, the name of the city of my God... and my new name" does not necessarily indicate three inscribed names. These phrases in Rev 3:12 may

---

[121] Beale, *The Book of Revelation*, 295.

[122] Aune, *Revelation 1-5*, 243.

refer to one name: the same name written upon the "white stone" of Rev 2:17. Ezekiel 48:35 records the name of the new Jerusalem as "the LORD is there," which may be translated, "the LORD is its name."[123] Similarly in Matthew 1:23 Jesus is named Immanuel: "God with us."

Charge to Heed the Word

The letter to the church in Philadelphia ends with the same charge found at the end of the other letters. This charge in Rev 3:13 extends the encouragements and promises issued to the faithful Philadelphians to all persevering believers. Every Christian who suffers from unjust persecutors can be sure that he or she will finally be vindicated. Every Christian can be sure that he or she will be kept from the worst affliction: the full outpouring of God's wrath. Every Christian is assured promises like those given to the church in Philadelphia. But this charge to heed the word would have been especially crucial for the church in Philadelphia to hear as they were in the very midst of unjust persecution.

---

[123] Beale, *The Book of Revelation*, 294.

Chapter Ten

Letter to the Church in Laodicea (Rev 3:14-22)

14 And write to the angel of the church in Laodicea:

The Amen, the faithful and true witness, the beginning of the creation of God, says these things:

15 I know your works, that you are neither cold nor hot. It would be fitting if you were cold or hot! *16* Consequently, because you are tepid– neither hot nor cold– I am about to vomit you out from my mouth. *17* Because you say,[124] "I am wealthy," and, "I have become rich," and, "I need nothing," and you don't know that you are wretched,[125] pathetic, destitute, blind, and naked. *18* I advise you to buy from me: gold refined by fire, that you

---

[124] The second ὅτι in this verse is left untranslated, because it is used to mark a quote– something that is accomplished in English through puntuation.

[125] As previously mentioned, several occurrences of the word καὶ are left untranslated because where Greek tends to separate all items in a list with a καὶ, English normally uses commas.

may be rich; white clothes, that you may clothe yourself so the shame of your nakedness might not be exposed; and eye salve in order to anoint your eyes so that you may see. *19* I lecture and I discipline whosoever I love; therefore, become zealous and repent. *20* Behold! I have been standing at the door and I am knocking, if anyone shall hear my voice and shall open the door, I will come in to him, and I will dine with him and he with me. *21* The victor:[126] I will give to him to sit with me upon my throne, as I too conquered and sat with my Father upon his throne. *22* Let he who has an ear hear what the Spirit says to the churches.

Introduction of the Audience and the Author

Laodicea was destroyed in a terrible earthquake in A.D. 62, but refused Roman aid for rebuilding because the city was wealthy enough to rebuild itself and its citizens desired independence. Laodicea had three major sources of wealth: 1. Banking (similar to modern Swiss banks); there was a grand bank, which had walls lined with gold, and which was

---

[126] ὁ νικῶν is understood as a nominative absolute (Beale, *The Book of Revelation*, 310).

protected by an inner wall within the city; 2. Linen (fine clothing products); 3. Salve (the manufacture of medicinal products, such as eye and ear salve, made from zinc oxide that naturally occurred in the area). Laodicea had a problem with drinking water, which flowed into town from hot springs in the hills and was lukewarm by the time it reached town. Alternatively, water could be brought from Colossae in barrels, but it was likewise lukewarm when it reached town.[127]

ὁ ἀμήν, ὁ μάρτυς ὁ πιστὸς καὶ ἀληθινός (*ho amēn, ho martus ho pistos kai alēthinos*) "the Amen, the faithful and true witness" as a title for Christ is meant to contrast Jesus with the hypocritical Laodiceans. This title in Revelation 3:14 is meant to assure them that the assessment concerning their condition as contained in this letter is completely correct.

ἡ ἀρχὴ τῆς κτίσεως τοῦ θεοῦ (*hē archē tēs ktiseōs tou theou*) "the beginning of the creation of God" is conceptually similar to "the firstborn from the dead" in Rev 1:5 (another passage in which Jesus is called "the faithful witness).[128] The idea

---

[127] Daniel E. Hatfield, "Revelation 3:14-22" (classroom lecture notes, *22440–Greek Syntax and Exegesis*, Spring 2007).

[128] Thomas Schreiner, "Three Marks of a Dead Church," Revelation 3:14-21 (sermon, *Clifton Baptist Church*, 16 November 2008); accessed 27 December 2013; available from http://cliftonbaptist.org/sermons-and-audio/; Internet.

is that Jesus, as He ushered in the resurrection, ushers in the *new* creation of God. This title for Christ bears striking similarity with what was proclaimed of Him in Colossians 1:15-20, a passage that many scholars believe was originally part of an early Christian hymn.[129] If these scholars are correct, then the Laodicean church may have been familiar with the song, and this title for Christ would prompt them to think more deeply concerning the truth about which they had been singing. Part of the problem that Paul confronted in Colossae concerned a focus on externals (Col 2:16). In a different way, the Laodicean church was focused on external matters; in their case, the focus was on wealth versus the Colossians' focus on ceremonies and ascetic practices. In whatever way a person is tempted to focus on external matters, his or her vision is helped through a re-focus on Christ as above all things.

Condemnation of the Laodiceans' Tepidity and Pride

The most probable origin of the imagery for "neither cold nor hot" in Revelation 3:15-16 is mentioned in the historical note above. Cold

---

[129] Notice that this passage *explains* Christ being called the "beginning" with the idea that He is "the firstborn from the dead" (Col 1:18).

or hot water is useful. Cold water is useful for refreshment. Hot water is useful for boiling food or for cleaning. Just as salt– a very useful substance– becomes useless if it loses its salinity (cf. Matt 5:13), lukewarm water is practically useless unless a change occurs.

ἐμέσαι (*emesai*) "vomit" in Rev 3:16 is used as a figure of speech meaning "utterly reject." "In Lev 18:25, 28: 20:22, the expression 'to vomit' out of the land is used of the fate of the Canaanites upon entry into Palestine, and the potential fate of the Israelites themselves."[130] James 4:6 declares that "God opposes the proud," and Jesus' words in Rev 3:17 prove that the Laodiceans were full of misplaced pride. Due to their tepidity and pride, the Laodiceans were in danger of being "utterly rejected:" removed from God's blessings and opposed by God.

Admonition and Encouragement to the Laodiceans

Jesus admonishes the erring Laodiceans in Rev 3:18 using the verb συμβουλεύω (*sumbouleuō*) "I advise." Jesus could have used a stronger term like "warn" or "rebuke." Instead, He uses a fatherly mode of expression, which is continued in Rev 3:19. This should remind readers that God often

---

[130] Aune, *Revelation 1-5*, 258.

draws sinners to repentance through His kindness (Rom 2:4).

In Revelation 3:18, Jesus advises the Laodiceans to obtain three items from Him. Jesus uses the infinitive ἀγοράσαι "to buy" as a metaphor due to the Laodiceans' focus on wealth. The items Jesus mentions– "gold refined by fire," "white clothes," and "eye salve"– are related to the Laodiceans' particular sources of wealth.

χρυσίον πεπυρωμένον ἐκ πυρὸς (*chrusion pepurōmenon ek puros*) "gold refined by fire" is used due to the heavenly connection with "gold" in Revelation. (Notice the "golden sash" around Jesus' chest in Rev 1:13 and that the new Jerusalem in Rev 21:18 is made of "pure gold.") Here the "gold refined by fire" also draws on the Laodiceans' pride in their grand bank with its gold-lined walls. The Laodiceans say, "I am wealthy" when they are really spiritually destitute (Rev 3:17). Jesus' concern that the Laodiceans become rich must be understood in spiritual terms, reminding readers of Jesus' words (as recorded in Matt 6:4, 6, 18) of the heavenly rewards that the Father will bestow on His followers due to their secret "acts of righteousness." In contrast to the external pomp in which the Laodiceans were currently boasting, Jesus is concerned that they have an internal righteousness leading to heavenly reward.

ἱμάτια λευκα (*himatia leuka*) "white clothes" is used because "white" symbolizes righteousness in Revelation. Here the "white clothes" are also used as a contrast to the elegant black garments produced in Laodicea. Instead of clothing themselves in the wealth of this world, the Laodiceans needed to be focused on being clothed in Christ's righteousness. Without these "white clothes," the Laodiceans would remain shamefully naked, utterly lacking righteousness in God's sight.

κολλούριον ἐγχρῖσαι τοὺς ὀφθαλμούς σου (*kollourion enchrisai tous ophthalmous sou*) "eye salve in order to anoint your eyes" is used because in Revelation "eyes" consistently indicates a heavenly perspective. Jesus has "eyes like a flame of fire" (Rev 2:18). Again, the Lamb has "seven eyes, which are the sevenfold Spirit of God sent out into all the earth" (Rev 5:6). In Revelation 3:18, the "eye salve" also draws on the Laodiceans' pride in their medicinal products.[131] The Laodiceans were confident in their positive self-assessment, but they were blind to their true condition. Like the Sardians, they needed to "become vigilant" (Rev 3:2). Jesus had taught His disciples that the

---

[131] *The NET Bible* editors/translators note that the word used for "eye salve"– κολλούριον– literally means a roll of dough. The salve was a powder made into a paste-like substance and placed on the eyes. Readers may recall John 9:6 in which Jesus healed a man who had been blind from birth by means of mud made from His spit.

eye is the lamp of the body: a metaphor speaking of the way that a person's focus– his aims and intentions[132]– sets the course of his life (Matt 6:22-23). Instead of being focused on the things of this world, the Laodiceans should have a heavenly perspective and become focused on the kingdom of God and His righteousness (Matt 6:33).

ἐλέγχω (*elenchō*) "lecture" refers to "a verbal rebuke designed to bring a person to acknowledge his fault;" παιδεύω (*paideuō*) "discipline" accomplishes the same goal by means of an action.[133] As a loving father gives good gifts to his children (Matt 7:9-11), our heavenly Father gives good gifts to believers. Though children rarely perceive it at the time, these good gifts include discipline (Heb 12:5-11). In Rev 3:19, we see that God in Christ uses all appropriate means possible to rescue His erring children and restore them into a full, proper relationship with Him.[134]

εἰσελεύσομαι πρὸσ αὐτὸν καὶ δειπνήσω μετ αὐτοῦ καὶ αὐτὸς μετ εμοῦ (*eiseleusomai pros*

---

[132] Matthew Henry, *The Matthew Henry Study Bible*, 1506.

[133] Thomas, *Revelation 1-7*, 319. See Prov 3:12.

[134] Notice that in engaging believers in "lecture" and "discipline," Jesus is taking on roles properly assigned to God: He is engaging in divine activity. These are also, as noted above, *fatherly* activities. This kind of activity may help readers understand why Jesus, the promised "Son" of Isaiah 9:6, is also named "Everlasting Father" in that passage.

auton kai deipnēsō met autou kai autos met emou) "I will come in to him, and I will dine with him and he with me" is "an invitation not for the readers to be converted, but to renew themselves in a relationship that has already begun, as is apparent from v. 19."[135] Revelation 3:20 holds a present promise, but may also point forward to an eschatological reality, as a comparison with Luke 12:36-37 demonstrates. 'Opening the door' in this verse seems to be metaphorical for the 'becoming zealous and repenting' in the previous verse. Through casting off tepidity and pride, the Laodicean Christians bring themselves into joyful intimate fellowship with Christ.

Promise to the Victor

The idea of the enthronement of the saints was revealed as early as in Daniel 7:18, 27.[136] The revelation here is in keeping with the Lord's earlier words to the apostles, recorded in Luke 22:28-30. In Revelation 3:21, Jesus says that the victor will sit with Him on His throne. How many can sit upon a single throne at one time? As the ancient world knew of a *bisellium*– a throne that was a single piece of furniture with two seats– the image here should bring to mind one piece of furniture with

---

[135] Beale, *The Book of Revelation*, 308.

[136] Aune, *Revelation 1-5*, 261.

multiple seats.[137] The persevering Christian follows the example of Christ, "who for the joy that was set before Him endured the cross, despising the shame, and is set down at the right hand of the throne of God" (Heb 12:2). Not only do we follow His example, but we also get to share in His reward, being promised that we will get to sit on His throne with Him.

Charge to Heed the Word

"Let he who has an ear hear what the Spirit says to the churches" (Rev 3:22). This has been the refrain throughout these seven letters. We must take heed of what the Spirit says to the churches not just in these letters, but in the entire book of Revelation, and indeed in the entire Bible. The messages given to the seven churches contain many differences, given the different circumstances of the various churches, but there are some crucial similarities as well. Each of the letters focuses the churches on the identity and activity of the glorified Lord Jesus. The churches were to focus on glorifying Jesus. Our focus must likewise be on worshiping Jesus and making Him known.

---

[137] Ibid., 262.

Bibliography

Greek Text

Aland, Barbara, Kurt Aland, Johannes Karavidopoulos, Carlo M. Martini, and Bruce M. Metzger, eds. *The Greek New Testament*, 4th ed., rev. Stuttgart, Germany: United Bible Societies, 2001.

Grammars/Lexical Aids

Black, David Alan. *It's Still Greek to Me.* Grand Rapids: Baker Books, 1998.

Friberg, Timothy, Barbara Friberg, and Neva F. Miller. *Analytical Lexicon of the Greek New Testament.* Victoria, BC: Trafford Publishing, 2005.

Gingrich, F. Wilbur. *Shorter Lexicon of the Greek New Testament.* Revised by Frederick W. Danker. Chicago: University of Chicago Press, 1983.

Louw, Johannes P. and Eugene A. Nida. *Greek-English Lexicon of the New Testament, Based on Semantic Domains.* New York: United Bible Societies, 1989.

Mounce, William D. *Analytical Lexicon to the Greek New Testament.* Grand Rapids: Zondervan, 1993.

Mounce, William D. *Basics of Biblical Greek.* Grand Rapids: Zondervan, 2003.

Plummer, Robert L. *Greek Review (22410).* Version 3.2. Louisville: The Southern Baptist Theological Seminary, 2007.

Summers, Ray. *Essentials of New Testament Greek.* Revised by Thomas Sawyer. Nashville: Broadman & Holman, 1995.

Thayer, Joseph H. *Thayer's Greek-English Lexicon of the New Testament.* Grand Rapids: Baker Book House, 1977.

Commentaries

Aune, David E. *Revelation 1-5.* Word Biblical Commentary, vol. 52. Dallas: Word Books, 1997.

Beale, G.K. *The Book of Revelation.* The New International Greek Testament Commentary. Grand Rapids: Wm. B. Eerdmans Publishing Co., 1999.

Gregg, Steve. *Revelation: Four Views.* Nashville: Thomas Nelson Publishers, 1997.

Hamilton Jr., James M. *Revelation.* Wheaton: Crossway, 2012.

Jamieson, Robert, A.R. Fausset, and David Brown. *Commentary Critical and Explanatory* on the Whole Bible. [On-line.] Accessed 28 October 2013. Available from http://www. biblestudytools.com/commentaries/jamieson-fausset-brown/revelation/revelation-2.html. Digital book.

Osborne, Grant. *Revelation.* Grand Rapids: Baker Book House, 2002.

Thomas, Robert L. *Revelation 1-7.* An Exegetical Commentary. Chicago: Moody Press, 1992.

Study Bibles

Abraham, A. Kenneth, ed. *The Matthew Henry Study Bible.* Iowa Falls: World Bible Publishers, 1997.

Criswell, W.A., ed. *The Believer's Study Bible.* Nashville: Thomas Nelson Publishers, 1991.

Harris III, W. Hall. *The NET Bible.* Belarus: Biblical Studies Press, 2007.

MacArthur, John F. *The MacArthur Study Bible.* La Habra, CA: Thomas Nelson, 2006.

Sproul, R.C., ed. *The Reformation Study Bible.* Orlando, FL: Ligonier Ministries, 2005.

Lectures

Hatfield, Daniel E. "Revelation 2:8-11." Classroom lecture notes. *22440–Greek Syntax and Exegesis.* Spring 2007.

_____. "Revelation 2:12-17." Classroom lecture notes. *22440–Greek Syntax and Exegesis.* Spring 2007.

_____. "Revelation 2:18-29." Classroom lecture notes. *22440–Greek Syntax and Exegesis.* Spring 2007.

_____. "Revelation 3:1-6." Classroom lecture notes. *22440–Greek Syntax and Exegesis.* Spring 2007.

_____. "Revelation 3:7-13." Classroom lecture notes. *22440–Greek Syntax and Exegesis.* Spring 2007.

_____. "Revelation 3:14-22." Classroom lecture notes. *22440–Greek Syntax and Exegesis.* Spring 2007.

Sermons

Schreiner, Thomas. "Grace from the Father, Son, and Spirit." Revelation 1:1-8. Sermon, *Clifton Baptist Church*, 14 September 2008. Accessed 14 January 2014. Available from http://cliftonbaptist.org/sermons-and-audio/. Internet.

_____. "Trusting in the Son of Man," Revelation 1:9-20. Sermon, *Clifton Baptist Church*, 21 September 2008. Accessed 15 January 2014. Available from http://

cliftonbaptist.org/sermons-and-audio/. Internet.

_____. "Losing Our First Love," Revelation 2:1-7. Sermon, *Clifton Baptist Church*, 28 September 2008. Accessed 15 January 2014. Available from http:// cliftonbaptist.org/sermons-and-audio/. Internet.

_____. "Faith Unto Death," Revelation 2:8-11. Sermon, *Clifton Baptist Church*, 5 October 2008. Accessed 16 January 2014. Available from http://cliftonbaptist.org/ sermons-and-audio/. Internet.

_____. "Promises, Promises." Revelation 3:7-13. Sermon, *Clifton Baptist Church*. 9 November 2008. Accessed 1 January 2014. Available from http://cliftonbaptist.org/ sermons-and-audio/. Internet.

_____. "Three Marks of a Dead Church." Revelation 3:14-21. Sermon, *Clifton Baptist Church*. 16 November 2008. Accessed 27 December 2013. Available from http:// cliftonbaptist.org/sermons-and-audio/. Internet.

Other Works

Evans, Tony. *Between a Rock and a Hard Place*. Chicago: Moody Publishers, 2010.

Gentry, K.L. *Before Jerusalem Fell.* Tyler: Institute for Christian Economics, 1989.

Irenaeus. *Adversus Haereses*, 5.30.3. [On-line.] Accessed 28 October 2013. Available from http://www.ccel.org/ccel/schaff/anf01.ix.i.html. Digital book.

Schaff, Philip. *History of the Christian Church Volume 4*. [On-line.] Accessed 28 October 2013. Available from http://www.ccel.org/ccel/schaff/hcc4.i.xiv.v.html. Digital book.

INDEX OF SCRIPTURES CITED

Revelation (continued)

Revelation (continued)

10:9	10	*19:20-21*	24
11:3-7	62	*19:21*	85, 94
11:10	62, 122	*20:11-15*	113
11:17	28	*20:12*	113
12:12	122	*20:14*	75
13:8	113, 122	*20:15*	114
13:12	122	*21:1*	67
13:14	122	*21:2*	67, 125
14:6	122	*21:3*	67
15:3	28	*21:6*	27, 48
15:6	45	*21:8*	94
16:7	28	*21:10*	33, 125
16:14	28	*21:18*	132
17:1	10	*21:22*	28
17:2	122	*21:27*	114
17:3	33	*22*	5
17:8	113, 122	*22:1-2*	68
17:10	34 n43	*22:6*	10
19:6	28	*22:7*	5, 12
19:12	46, 87	*22:8*	10
19:13	24	*22:12*	66
19:15	28, 47	*22:13*	27
19:16	24	*22:15*	94
19:19	24	*22:16*	10, 48, 99